Hollywood Icons Vol. 3

Richard Burton and

Elizabeth Taylor

2 Books in 1

Katy Holborn

Copyright © 2017.

All rights reserved. No part of this publication may be reproduced, distributed, or transmitted in any form or by any means, including photocopying, recording, or other electronic or mechanical methods, without the prior written permission of the publisher, except in the case of brief quotations embodied in critical reviews and certain other noncommercial uses permitted by copyright law.

This book is intended for informational and entertainment purposes only. The publisher limits all liability arising from this work to the fullest extent of the law.

Richard Burton

A Richard Burton Biography

Katy Holborn

Table of Contents

Richard Burton – Beyond the Scandal

Introduction

Early Years

'A Spoiled Genius from the Welsh Gutter'

Rising Star

Hollywood Comes Calling

A Multimedia Star

On Film

The Best of Burton

On Television

On Radio

On the Stage

About a Scandal

Sybil Williams

Elizabeth Taylor

The "Liz & Dick" Show

Susan Hunt

Sally Hay

If Only

Richard Burton – Beyond the Scandal

Introduction

Liz & Dick and *"Le Scandale."*

It is unfortunate that a rare, generational talent's lifetime of achievements can be commonly, unjustly reduced to a few words. That one is remembered as a "fine actor but…," where mention of his talent is almost always trailed by that weighty contrasting conjunction - *but* he had a troubled personal life. *But* he consumed too much alcohol. *But* he courted scandal after scandal. *But* he had a wild streak.

Unfortunately, that is where the common memory of Richard Burton currently stands. Acclaimed actor of stage and screen, seven-time Oscar nominee, a Tony Award winner and Grammy Award winner, who had owned one of the greatest speaking voices the world has ever heard and committed to tape and film – is usually most memorable by his weaknesses and his ill-fated, great love affair.

Granted, that is the nature of a "scandal." The word derives from the Greek, *skandalon*, the trigger of a trap that causes something or someone to fall; and the Late Latin *scandalum* which means 'stumbling block.' Scandal, therefore, is that which causes someone to fall – to be discredited.

And so, it is taken for granted what is meant when Richard Burton is described as a great actor; just as it is easy to forget that his infamous partner-in-(moral)-crime, Elizabeth Taylor, had also been very good at their craft. The blinding flashes of tabloid culture that captured their every move, ironically showed false images. The pictures derail from an accurate memory, obscuring it behind the false light of distracting after-images. There is so much more to Richard Burton than a failed love affair. He had a life before "*Le Scandale,*" and one after it. He had a life *beyond* it.

Richard Burton was a coal miner's son who went to Oxford and became one of the greatest Shakespearean actors of his time. He had his demons – a penchant for drink and women, the occasional cruel tongue, a kind of wildness - but he had a love of books and a gift for words, mixing Shakespeare and intelligent conversation with wit and self-deprecating humor. He was charming and generous. He was a compelling actor to watch and listen to. He had intelligence, intensity and rakish appeal. He wasn't just handsome, he was magnetic.

He was so much more than the parasitic scandal that has become to be attached to him, sucking on the lifeblood of what should be a more vital, more fitting memory. A man, after all, should not be remembered solely for his biggest – even if it they are also his most beautiful – mistakes.

Early Years

'A Spoiled Genius from the Welsh Gutter'

Richard Walter Jenkins was born on the 10th of November, 1925, in Pontrhydyfen, a South Wales mining town. He was the 12th of 13 children by Richard "Dic" Walter and wife Edith Jenkins, who died of puerperal fever after giving birth to number 13. Richard Burton was only two when he lost his 44-year-old mother in 1927. His father, who worked in the mines, was a drinker and gambler allegedly not disinclined to violence. He was also often away. Given that his father was not the ideal guardian, Burton was taken in by his older sister Cecilia and her husband, Elfed, who looked after him at their home in Port Talbot. He found support in another one of his siblings, Ifor, a father figure at 19 years his senior, who would later often be by his side as his personal assistant.

Richard Burton did well in school and got a scholarship to Port Talbot Secondary School when he was 11 years old. During his youth, he showed interest and promise in a lot of things. He was a good student and did well in both English and Welsh literature, though he came from a predominantly Welsh-speaking home. He had talent for speaking and singing too, and had once been awarded an Eisteddfod prize for soprano (Eisteddfod is a long-running festival celebrating the art and culture of Wales). He appeared in school stage performances. He was also accomplished in sports, particularly rugby and cricket. He later became a member of the Air Traffic Corps.

His multitude of interests and pursuits wouldn't keep him in school steadily, however. By some accounts, he left school at the age of 15 and became a restless and dissatisfied assistant at a haberdashery. At 16, he reportedly worked in a wartime cooperative, trading coupons and supplies. Even at his young age, Richard was already independent. But another notable thing about him in his mid-teens is that he was already consistent in some of the vices and habits that would later be associated with him as a star; he enjoyed cigarettes, alcohol and women.

Meredith Jones, the founder of a local youth center Richard Burton went to as well as being his schoolmaster, saw him for his potential and swooped in for her own brand of academic rescue. She prevailed upon the

Glamorgan Education Committee to let him re-enter grammar school. He returned as arranged, and would benefit from the kind attentions of another educator who would champion his potential – a man named Philip Burton.

Philip was a teacher, as well as Richard's commanding officer in the Port Talbot squadron of the Air Training Corps. Like Meredith Jones, Philip Burton saw something in the young Richard that compelled him to be proactive in the young man's development. He saw Richard's energy and enthusiasm, his voracious appetite for reading and especially for poetry. Richard was by then in school performances as well as those of a local youth drama group.

Philip, seeing Richard's passion and potential, became active in helping him develop his talents. He nurtured the promising young man's interest in literature and the performing arts, and under Philp's wing, Richard blossomed. That famous Burton Voice, for example, was partly attributed to mountain treks and spouting Shakespeare from great heights – to improve projection!

Philip Burton had a lot to work with in his young protégé, however, for some of Richard's talents were God-given and self-developed. The Jenkins family was said to have been known for their beautiful voices after all, with the quality of *"coal dust and rain,"* as the ever-articulate Burton himself had once described it. Sunday services were also instrumental to how he developed his oratorical skills; he spent hours attuned to preachers at church. As a critical fan of film, he also recognized how having a distinct manner of speaking could be integral to the making of a star – this was probably why he had been so willing to be molded by his mentor's grueling methods. All in all, Richard Burton understood the power of a good voice, and he had both the raw talent and willingness to do hard work to achieve it. Together, Philip and Richard made the younger man's voice louder, and worked on softening his Welsh accent.

Richard eventually attained a school certificate, and found an opportunity to study in Exeter College at Oxford. It was for a special six-month term for an air force cadet with obligations of later military service. But to be able to have a better chance of becoming an undergraduate at the prestigious institution after he is demobilized (that is, to be freed from active service as would be the case after the war), Philip Burton was advised to adopt Richard. Legal issues reportedly prevented this, but Philip could still take the teenager in as a legal ward, which he did. Thus, Richard Walter Jenkins became: Richard Burton, named for his mentor.

In his later years, the intelligent, well-spoken actor was firmly aware of his reputation, and he conceded it with his signature wit. He had described it as "*…that of a spoiled genius from the Welsh gutter…*" Indeed, there was something about the young Richard Burton - his smarts, a spark comparable to genius – that simply shone and inspired others to take up his cause, care for him and help him succeed.

As shown by Meredith Jones and Philip Burton, something about Richard simply made people stop and take notice. They wouldn't be alone in this. Even before his time in Oxford gave him gravitas, he was already garnering praise for his performances. His first outing as a professional on the stage was for Emlyn Williams' *The Druid's Rest* in 1943, which he performed in Liverpool. It was a success and made its way to London in 1944, where his performance moved a critic on the *New Statesman* magazine to say the young actor had *"exceptional ability."* Those two words proved powerful for a young man on his first real acting job; it has been credited for strengthening his commitment to continue the pursuit of acting.

More experience and opportunities followed, most notably a performance of Shakespeare while he was studying in Oxford. As Angelo in *Measure for Measure*, he was to perform a big role by The Bard before a distinguished audience who would one day shape his future. Among them was influential West End theater manager and producer, Binkie Beaumont, who told Burton to get in touch with him post-war if he wanted to pursue acting as a career.

The fiery young man took him up on that offer after World War II.

Rising Star

Richard Burton joined the Royal Air Force in 1944, and though he had too poor an eyesight to be classified as a pilot, he did become a navigator. World War II came to an end before he got any combat experience, but demobilization did not come right away and he was on the force until 1947, with time in service broken briefly for acting work, such as in in 1946, when Philip Burton helped him get a leave for *The Corn is Green* (1946), a television adaptation of the play by Emlyn Williams. He played Morgan Evans, a promising, working-class student in a Welsh mining community, upon whom a proactive new transplant, his school teacher Miss Moffatt, latches her hopes and invests her efforts.

The play was based on the Welshman playwright and actor, Emlyn Williams' own rise from a working-class community. The role of a devoted educator in setting a promising student on the right path, mirrored some of Richard Burton's own experiences. Williams and Burton worked together on several projects, and the older Williams would also be instrumental in shaping Burton's career. His play, *The Corn is Green* would be a particularly important one for other members of the Burton family though; in the 2000s, a production would feature Richard's daughter, Kate, playing Miss Moffatt on stage opposite her son, Morgan Ritchie - in the role once played by his grandfather.

Richard Burton left the RAF in 1947 and settled down in London to pursue an acting career. He really did take up Binkie Beaumont on the offer made from his Oxford days, and locked down a contract where he was paid even when he wasn't actively working. At £500 per year, he was reportedly already earning more than his family had ever seen in their lifetime.

He worked in radio plays for a while but by 1948 he was making his debut on screens with *The Last Days of Dolwyn* (also known by the title, *Women of Dolwyn*). The drama by Emlyn Williams (and the only film he would direct) is set in a small, quiet village in North Wales, whose residents are looking at an imminent end to the only life they know in the place they love. A powerful company plans to build a dam nearby, that would flood and ultimately destroy it. It is capitalism versus conscience, and explores the costs of development... complicated by an embittered former local who is determined to see the community fall. Standing up to these forces are an elderly woman and her adopted son, Gareth – a role said to have been written by Williams with Burton in mind. He was delightful in it.

Aside from writer / director Emlyn Williams, who believed Burton would be a success in the industry, and the critics and audiences that enjoyed his performance, another person would find Richard Burton magnetic – his *The Last Days of Dolwyn* co-star, Sybil Williams. Like Burton, Sybil hailed from Wales. She was 19 when they met while filming and he, 23. The beautiful young couple married in 1949.

The Last Days of Dolwyn would be Sybil's only movie credit (she would trail her husband's red-hot career across two continents during their marriage), but it was just the beginning for Richard Burton. In the short period between 1949 to 1951, he would appear in *Now Barabbas Was a Robber* (1949), *Waterfront Women* (1950; also known as *Waterfront*), *Her Panelled Door* (1950; also known by the title, *The Woman with No Name*) and *Green Grow the Rushes* (1951). For *The Woman with No Name*, he had reportedly earned as much as £1,000 for ten days of work. He was clearly an actor to watch, but not just on screen. In the early 1950s, Richard Burton was also making headway into dominance of the stage.

He was in the Christopher Fry verse play, *The Lady's Not for Burning* (1949), which later made its way before receptive American audiences in New York – it was Burton's first taste of the New York stage. In 1950, he was also in the plays, *A Phoenix Too Frequent*; and *The Boy with the Cart* in England. He was the lead actor for the latter, and was spotted by actor / director, Anthony Quayle, who then tapped the young talent for productions of *Henry IV* and *Henry V* at Stratford-upon-Avon, during the Festival of Britain's Shakespeare season of 1951. Critics were bowled over. According to one such critic, Burton's performance "*…turned interested speculation into awe…*" Soon, whispers were circulating about the arrival of a man who could very well be the next Laurence Olivier.

Hollywood Comes Calling

Hollywood, as it does, soon came calling on the gifted young actor. By 1952, he had signed with director and producer, Alexander Korda on a multi-year contract of £100 a week. He would juggle a hectic schedule between stage and screen. Shakespeare and the London stage had a distinct command of his time in the 1950s –

Burton was in performances of *The Tempest, Hamlet, King John, Twelfth Night, Coriolanus* and *Othello*. He was highly in demand and did other theater work too, though. He returned to Broadway briefly in 1951 to do *Legend of Lovers*; he did *Montserrat* back in London in 1952; and another stint in New York for *Time Remembered* (1957), which gave him a Tony nomination for Best Actor in a Play … all this, while pursuing his craft in other media.

Unfortunately, his success also meant he had plenty of access to the habits and vices he had enjoyed since his early teenage days – smoking and drinking. His signature voice may have even been partly due to his hardcore smoking. Contemporary actor Dominic West (famous for HBO hit, *The Wire*), for example, was slated to depict

Richard Burton in a BBC biopic. He found success depicting the Burton voice only after a night of heavy drinking and smoking.

Vices aside, onwards Burton went toward the inevitable fate of a handsome, talented young man with intelligence, charisma and grit – stardom. But it was a stardom not just on stage and screen but also on television and radio. And Burton wouldn't just do it in one continent, but two.

A Multimedia Star

Of stardom, Richard Burton had once said, *"you reach the top of the heap, but it's a circle, and you slip on the down side…"*

This is what being on "top of the heap" looks like for a man of Burton's talents: his body of work comprised a tapestry of achievements, each woven into the other. In film, television, radio and theater his credits lie, in the United Kingdom and the United States, at tangled points of time.

On Film

His extensive theater resume of the 1950s is interwoven with his initial forays into Hollywood. His launching, via *My Cousin Rachel* (1953), was a bold one. It was only his film debut in the United States, yet he was already appearing in a drama based on a work by famed novelist, Daphne Du Maurier, as the leading man opposite established actress Olivia de Havilland. There are varying accounts on how he was brought into the project. Some say it is via director George Cukor, who had originally been slated to direct the project until he was ousted following clashes with the producer. Others say it was the popular writer, Du Maurier herself, who had recommended him for the part. Either way, Richard Burton made it count; he got his first Academy Award nomination (albeit in the Supporting category) and a Golden Globe for Most Promising Newcomer, in his first Hollywood role:

- *My Cousin Rachel* **(1953).** In this film, Richard Burton plays Philip Ashley, who inherits his late cousin Ambrose's estate – over Ambrose's wife, Rachel. He juggles a growing attraction for her with suspicions that she may have had something to do with Ambrose's death.

Richard Burton was highly prolific in the 1950s. Aside from the plays he did in London and New York during the decade, he also did a lot on film in the U.K. and the U.S. He followed up *My Cousin Rachel* with three films under a deal with 20th Century Fox – *Desert Rats* (1953) and *The Robe* (1953). He received his second Oscar nomination for his work in the latter:

- *The Robe* **(1953).** The epic, based on a New York Times yearlong bestseller by

Lloyd Douglas, made history as the first movie filmed in CinemaScope. It was large both in literal scale (the new technology showed wide) and in content (it was a biblical tale) – as well as in box office receipts. Here, Richard Burton plays Marcellus, a self-indulgent Roman guard who plays a part in the crucifixion of Jesus, leading him to haunting realizations and eventually, redemption in the Christian underground.

If *My Cousin Rachel* made American audiences pay attention, *The Robe* made him a star. More film work naturally followed. In lavishly shot and fairly entertaining *The Rains of Ranchipur* (1955), Burton played Dr. Rama Safti, an ex-freedom fighter caught in the cross-hairs of Lana Taylor's man-eating, married heiress. He was in *Prince of Players* (1955), the biopic of Edwin Booth, the brother of Abraham Lincoln's assassin. As Edwin Booth, who had been an actor not unlike himself, Burton unleashed parts of Shakespeare's *Hamlet*, *Romeo and Juliet* and *Othello* with ease. The following year, he was in the title role of the epic, *Alexander the Great* (1956). He also appeared in *Sea Wife* (1957) and *Bitter Victory* (1957).

Richard Burton was making bank, and by the late 1950s, it was time for a few major changes. He moved to Celigny, Switzerland, for more favorable taxes on his considerable income. His wife, Sybil, would also give birth to their daughter, Kate, and Kate would be followed by Jessica in 1960.

Burton was highly productive in this decade, but not many of the films he made were particularly well-regarded. The movies that would constitute the best of his work wouldn't come until later in his career, though he did cap off the 1950s with an impressive turn in the kitchen sink drama, *Look Back in Anger*:

- ***Look Back in Anger* (1959)**. "Kitchen sink" is a term that has been used for art focused on the experiences of working class urbanites, often with an "angry young man" at its center. This kind of realism in drama was particularly in vogue in the United Kingdom during the 1950s and 1960s, after post-war reforms saw more educated writers and artists with working class backgrounds helping shape the culture of the day. As Jimmy Porter, Richard Burton is compelling in alternating states of aggression and vulnerability – an angry young man, indeed. Jimmy is an educated, part-time musician from the working class, whose marriage with a woman from the upper-classes, Alison, suffers from his ill-controlled anger.

The Best of Burton

As an actor, he has 79 television and movie credits to his name. Some of them have become well-loved classics, others forgotten failures, others yet were unremarkable outings or jobs he had taken on just for financial reasons. It's a thick filmography either way, with a number of must-see films that showcase the Welshman at his best. Aside from *The Robe* and *Look Back in Anger* earlier mentioned, the following movies are considered stand-outs in his resume:

- *Cleopatra* **(1963)** is famous for being (1) the film that made Liz & Dick and "*Le Scandale*" possible; (2) a cautionary tale of Hollywood production nightmares; and (3) being a financial disappointment. That said – the film is essential Richard Burton viewing in his turn as Mark Anthony to his real-life lover, Elizabeth Taylor's Cleopatra. Their on-screen chemistry sizzles, and the film is a handsome one, which would win four out of nine Academy Award nominations.

- *Becket* **(1964).** Peter Glenville's *Becket* is adapted from Jean Anouilh play and features Richard Burton in the title role facing off against Peter O'Toole's King Henry II. The King has appointed his close friend Thomas Becket as Lord Chancellor and Archbishop of Canterbury, expecting loyalty and deference by the church to the state. They feud – lethally - when Becket instead finds spirituality and courage to challenge the King.

- *Richard Burton's Hamlet* **(1964).** Not everyone had the chance to see and hear and experience the electricity of Richard Burton on a live stage. For the next best thing, this film is a recording of Richard Burton's minimalist Hamlet, from a public performance of the 1964 Broadway production.

- *The Night of the Iguana* **(1964)** saw Richard Burton taking on a Tennessee Williams' play, in this adaptation with director John Huston. The film features Burton as a defrocked priest and alcoholic, wrestling inner demons and caught in sexual tension with Deborah Kerr and Ava Gardner in a Mexican coastal town. It was a commercial and critical hit which landed four Academy Award nominations – none of which were for Richard Burton, even if the film is believed to be Burton at his best.

- *The Spy Who Came In from the Cold* **(1965).** Based on a John Le Carre thriller, Richard Burton is nuanced and riveting as Alec Lemas, a world-weary, burn-out spy at the tail end of his career when he is given a dangerous assignment that could be a trap for a larger agenda.

- ***Who's Afraid of Virginia Woolf?* (1966).** The collection of films made by Richard Burton and Elizabeth Taylor could be a really mixed bag, but here, they are both unforgettable in Mike Nichols' debut offering, an adaptation of the Edward Albee play. As George and Martha, a married couple mired in alcohol and disappointment in each other, they host a young couple and horrify them over an evening of escalating displays of hurt and anger. Both he and then-wife Liz would be nominated for an Oscar, but it is the lady of the house who brings the statuette home.

- ***Where Eagles Dare* (1968)**. *Where Eagles Dare* is the result of Richard Burton's search for a hit after a string of misses. He and his then-wife, Elizabeth Taylor, had a lavish lifestyle with a high price tag, and he needed a traditional blockbuster. The benchmark was perhaps something like *The Guns of Navarone* (1961). Burton worked with friend and producer Elliot Kastner, who then tapped into the talents of novelist Alistair MacLean, upon whose work *The Guns of Navarone* had been based. The famous novelist churned out a screenplay in just six weeks – *Where Eagles Dare*, which he would also turn into a book. The film was popular, and though a few critics bemoaned a great actor like Richard Burton "selling out," *Where Eagles Dare* was generally favorably received. It was a thriller with twists and turns, and plenty of action, fight sequences, and breathtaking stunt work.

In this big-budget World War II spy thriller, Richard Burton plays British officer, Major John Smith, who is in charge of a team of Allied commandos tasked with the rescue of a valuable American general imprisoned in a Nazi stronghold. Amongst them is an American soldier played by Clint Eastwood, who was by then, a star on the rise after a number of hit spaghetti westerns.

- ***Under Milk Wood* (1972).** The Burton Voice is in full force here, a screen version of the celebrated work written by the late Dylan Thomas. Thomas had been highly admired by Richard Burton and the two Welshmen were friends. They were heard together in the late-1940s for *In*

Parenthesis, a BBC adaptation of the war poem by David Jones. It was a treasured experience by Burton, who was then an unknown talent and had but a small part. Dylan Thomas' death from alcoholic poisoning in November, 1953 at the age of 39 was reportedly devastating to Richard Burton, whose voice would be very instrumental in keeping Dylan Thomas' works alive. He presented a Dylan Thomas tribute for television in 1962; and performed a number of Dylan Thomas' works for radio, including *Under Milk Wood* in 1954 shortly after Thomas passed away.

Under Milk Wood, described as a *"play for voices,"* is a classic that has found its way onto the arts in many incarnations – play, jazz album, opera, ballet – and in film via this early-1970s interpretation of Andrew Sinclair with Richard Burton, Elizabeth Taylor and Peter O'Toole starring. The whimsical, endearing play is about a day in the sleepy Welsh fishing village, Llareggub, and the memories, thoughts and interactions of its quirky (living and dead!) community.

Andrew Sinclair was an untested director when he landed the casting coup of the two superstars. It was Peter O'Toole, a friend from before they were famous, who connected him to Taylor and Burton. Years later, Sinclair shared his experience filming with the larger-than-life pair; Elizabeth had many specific demands on her wardrobe and schedule; and Richard

Burton would drink, yes, but remained "*a supreme professional*" save for the bloodshot eyes they had to shoot around. They were both gracious enough to send him notes of thanks. The film was not a financial success, though it is believed by some that it wasn't necessarily intended to be. Some believe it was a tax write-off; then again, Richard Burton always had a strong attachment to the words of Dylan Thomas. It has even been said that Burton was buried with Dylan Thomas' poetry.

- *Equus* **(1977)**. The 1970s weren't particularly kind to Richard Burton, whose films have become less remarkable. But he continued working and churned out a marvelous performance for *Equus*, a psychological thriller. The movie is director Sidney Lumet's adaptation of the disquieting Peter Shaffer play of the same title. In *Equus*, Burton, a world-weary psychiatrist, is charged with the case of an unbalanced stable hand who mutilated a number of horses. In the course of digging into the boy's demons, he finds himself fighting against his own.

Burton was great in the film, after all, he must have had a lot of practice; he'd played the role of psychiatrist Martin Dysart before. In 1976, he returned to Broadway after a long absence, drawn in by the Peter Shaffer play. He was so impressed by the work that he said it was *"the most exceptional"* he'd encountered in years, and that he could play that part, "*any time, any place.*" He did not even care that he did not originate the part, as could have been expected by a star of his standing (he was preceded by *Psycho's* Anthony Perkins, and Welsh actor Anthony Hopkins who was then being hailed as the "new" Richard Burton!). He was simply compelled to play it, and compelled to return to the Broadway stage, lest he not have an opportunity to do so again. He was so invested in the part that he sobered up (with the help of as young new girlfriend, Suzy Hunt), and even had changes made on Dysart's costume – he wore his own rumpled, lived-in suit that he felt was more appropriate to the character.

The film came shortly after the play. At the time he had signed up to appear on the stage for *Equus*, he had no guarantees of being in the film version, which was already in the works at that time. Among the actors in consideration for the meaty part were Marlon Brando and Jack Nicholson. But the role did go to him, and Burton was brilliant in it. By some accounts, Sidney Lumet locked down all of the character Martin Dysart's monologues in one productive day of filming.

Burton received his final Academy Award nomination for his efforts here. He wouldn't win, but he did bring home a Golden Globe for Best Actor in a Motion Picture - Drama.

- *Nineteen Eighty-Four* **(1984).** Despite the faulty and / or forgettable pictures that would liberally pepper his filmography, Richard Burton made his exit on a grand, high note with this film adaptation of George Orwell's dystopian novel.

   The story is set in a totalitarian state controlled by a small group of powerful people, the Inner Party and their figurehead, Big Brother, who assert their agenda and restrictive vision of the state through constant supervision, propaganda, conformity and suppression of the rest of the population. The film is centered on Winston Smith (played by John Hurt), a kind of average man with an inconsequential life – until his illegal thoughts and restlessness find an outlet in a subversive love affair, counter to the ideals of the state.

Richard Burton plays the sinister O'Brien, an esteemed member of the Inner Party, who takes on the rehabilitation of Winston into a person more aligned with the ideals of the state. He employs teaching and torture, a kind of father figure with a sadistic streak. It was Richard Burton's final role. He was in pain and somewhat ill during the production, and would pass away a couple of months prior to the film's release. He was unfortunately no longer around to bask in the success and acclaim it would bring his name.

On Television

The medium of television experienced rapid growth in years following World War II. More and more homes started to own them, and technology allowed for larger coverage and availability of programming. In the United Kingdom for example, television ownership grew aggressively from the time statistics were collected in 1956 (when it was found that one in three households had at least one television) to the 1970s, where ownership of a TV at home was at 93%. Like many of his peers then, Richard Burton shared his talents with the increasingly popular medium.

He has credits on a wide range of movies, series and specials. He read poetry, prose and parts of Shakespeare for use in various programming, including children's shows and documentaries. He also brought many plays to life on television. In *The Lady's Not for Burning* (1950), for example, he appeared in the TV adaptation of a play he'd done on the stage. He would also do Shakespeare's *The Tempest* (1960) and John Osbourne's *A Subject of Scandal and Concern* (1960), where he received critical praise for his depiction of George Holyoake, who was the last person accused of blasphemy and placed under trial for speaking publicly of atheism in England.

Burton did TV adaptations of novels, such as Earnest Hemingway's *The Fifth Column* (1960); and in *The DuPont Show of the Month* (1957), he did a turn as Heathcliff for an adaptation of Emily Bronte's *Wuthering Heights*. He also did TV biopics, such as in *Wagner* (1983), and he played Winston Churchill twice - for a 26-episode series in

1960 (*Winston Churchill: The Valiant Years*) and a film in 1974 (*Walk with Destiny*).

He presented a tribute to his beloved hero and friend, the late poet Dylan Thomas in 1962. In 1973, he and Elizabeth Taylor teamed up for *Divorce His – Divorce Hers*, about the deterioration of an 18-year marriage. It sounds too close to home, but the Burtons proved no stranger to treading the line between fact and fiction. They've done so before and will do so again.

Richard Burton and Elizabeth Taylor were incredibly beautiful and glamorous, for example, while hilariously playing a version of themselves in the episode, "Lucy Meets the Burtons" in *Here's Lucy* (1970). The season three premiere was a big ratings draw, and in it, "Richard Burton" evades fans by donning a plumber's uniform. Lucy naturally mistakes him for one and dragoons him into service. Things get complicated when she finds and tries on one of Elizabeth Taylor's diamond rings in his belongings and it gets stuck on her finger, where it stays, even as an important press appearance scheduled for the Burtons is approaching and the ring is expected to be on display. Hilarity ensues as Lucy and the Burtons try to bull their way through the event. A few choice lines riffed on the controversial couple's public image, among them:

- *"Champagne is good for everything – I wash my hair in it"* ("Elizabeth Taylor" suggests a way of removing the ring from Lucy's finger);
- *"And they call me a two-fisted drinker"* ("Richard Burton" commenting on a toast he makes with his wife and Lucy); and

- *"It almost makes up for not winning the Oscar"* ("Richard Burton" on being included in a Bus Tour of Movie Star homes, unseating the likes of Liberace).

And of course Richard Burton often appeared on television as his actual self (rather than the "character" of "As Himself"), in interviews discussing for his projects, or in features about his craft, his colleagues, his life, and his proud roots in Wales. Other notable appearances include *Alice in Wonderland* (1983), an adaptation of the Eva LaGallienne stage production; and *Ellis Island* (1984), a mini-series on immigrants coming to the United States in the early twentieth century. In both projects, he starred alongside his daughter, Kate Burton - a hardworking and accomplished actress with achievements all on her own.

She currently has over 80 movie and television credits, and is best known to contemporary audiences for recurring, scene-stealing roles on hit shows like *Scandal* and *Grey's Anatomy*.

Ellis Island was Richard Burton's last television role and it was aired after his death.

On Radio

Richard Burton was a handsome man, and a great actor who could convey a range of emotions. But even by sound alone, he is able to captivate. But how can one describe the sound and style of one of the greatest speakers to ever walk the earth?

"The Burton Voice," as it would come to be known, was such a treasure that, in the words of one critic, it could have given *"an air of verse to a recipe for stewed hare."* According to Andrew Sinclair, who had directed Burton in *Under Milk Wood*, it was a voice that seemed to embody humankind's 'passions and powers' such that listening to Burton *"…was to listen to the human condition."*

Richard Burton's voice is so singular it is as individual as a fingerprint. And like a fingerprint, it is inlaid with grooves of his personality and history. From the actor's roots, it had a Welsh mining town's 'coal, dust and rain.' From his time trekking up mountains to spout Shakespeare and the Bible from its heights, it was a voice of power and projection. It rang with notes of hangovers and smoke. It is beyond describing, though many have been moved to flowery language by trying. Luckily, the world is flush with recordings of Richard Burton's signature talent and many of us can simply listen and marvel, and attempt to find words for it ourselves. He had fortunately been generous with it.

Richard Burton had a long and fruitful relationship with BBC Radio – from the start of his career toward the end of his life, he was active in lending them his talents, for fees that would have been but a small slice of what he could have earned instead if he had spent his time on film or television or theater. This has been attributed to his love of language; sporadically from the late-1940s to the early-1980s, he could be heard on radio reading plays, prose and poetry.

On the Stage

Thanks to technology, we have the opportunity to hear many publicly available recordings of Richard Burton. Some are said to be lost, like that of his first effort at *In Parenthesis* with Dylan Thomas in the late-1940s, but there are still plenty to behold and enjoy. But what magic could it have been to see and hear him live, at his best? He had, after all, often described himself as a stage actor.

Compared to the previous years, there was less to be seen of Richard Burton on the stage during the 1960s through to the 1980s. Whenever he was there, though, he created a splash. He was in *Camelot* (1960), where he played King Arthur opposite Julie Andrews as Guinevere. He would bring home a Tony Award for Best Actor in a Musical for his good work.

In 1964, he was Hamlet in the Shakespeare play, which would see him get a Tony nomination for Best Actor in a Play. One of the live performances was recorded, screened across America, and is of course, thankfully available to contemporary audiences on video. It was by all accounts a successful endeavor, but for a miscellany of reasons, he wouldn't return to Broadway until 1976 for *Equus*, playing psychiatrist Martin Dysart. His performance in the play preceded his acquisition of the role for the later film and was in a sense, an "audition." The part was a meaty one, with actors like Marlon Brando and Jack Nicholson reportedly under consideration for it. Burton's successful stage outing is the factor that likely edged out the competition.

Equus was followed up by another run for *Camelot* in 1980. His final play was *Private Lives* (1983) – which is notable for, aside from being his last turn on stage, being a reunion with his controversial, larger-than-life, former flame, Elizabeth Taylor (but more on this, later).

Richard Burton had such stage presence. He called this "*intangible*" quality of actors, "*the ability to 'take stage'."* He attributed it to a combination of factors, among them "*sex or power,*" and reportedly realized he had it when he was a "*nobody name*" at the age of 25. As he was born in 1925, that would have been around 1950, when he was doing *The Lady's Not for Burning*. He'd been professionally appearing on stage for years by then, however (his first was in Emlyn Williams' *Druid's Rest* in 1943, and he had already been hailed as a promising talent), so it is somewhat surprising that he should have just realized it at that age. Another thing that is somewhat surprising about Richard Burton is that he had admitted to 'sweating and shaking in the wings.' He was also known to smoke a lot of cigarettes to calm his nerves. But who would have known it, with this stage actor's gift for drawing in an audience.

About a Scandal

Of the things that were lovable about the theater, Richard Burton said he liked applause and indeed, he must have received quite a lot of it from the captivated audiences of his stage work. But Burton would draw in an altogether different kind of audience when he took up an affair with the impossibly beautiful star, Elizabeth Taylor.

From the spotlight and klieg lights of stage and film, he became captive to the flashing lights of paparazzi cameras. He and Taylor were turned into characters – lustful, wild, love-consumed, indulgent, condemned – and their lives turned into a story for all the world to see: one the greatest love affairs of all time.

Sybil Williams

Before Richard Burton was the "Dick" half of the notorious "Liz & Dick," he was in a marriage of fourteen years as husband to Sybil Williams. Sybil was born in Tylorstown, Rhondda Valley in 1929. Like Burton, she was Welsh, with a family involved in mining. Her father was a coal mine official. She was orphaned early at the age of 15 and, again like Burton, came to live with an older sister. She studied at the London Academy of Music and Dramatic Arts, and met Richard Burton on her first movie, *Women of Dolwyn* (1949), where she had a small part.

Love and marriage came swiftly. Within months, they were wed. She was just 20 years old at the time but they were both young, with Burton himself just in his early

20s. Sybil quickly found herself the wife of a swiftly rising star, and she would ultimately be trailing after him wherever his work and commitments took them. She told *The New York Times* in 1994 that she did not think it was a sacrifice of her own prospects, however. As a matter of fact, one of her treasured memories of their turbulent time together was when she sailed, New York-bound on the *Queen Mary*, with "*the golden boy.*" She reveled in the warmth of adventure and promise, as one of 'two Welsh kids traveling first class.'

His work took him to many places, but eventually the couple settled down in Switzerland, with a villa at Celigny along Lake Geneva. They also stated a family, having daughter Kate in 1957, and Jessica in 1960. It sounds idyllic, but it was by no means so. Even before his affair with Elizabeth Taylor, Richard Burton already had a wandering eye with a reputation as a ladies' man. He was admired for his looks and talent, but also for his generosity, intelligence, wit and charm. His appreciation for literature and devotion to the written word made him fascinating too. All of these things together made for a very magnetic man, and he was not bashful about employing his talents. He could bust out poetry and Shakespeare, and can wow with a Welsh song. He was as able to impress anonymous, attractive women (it is said he was available for a romp with random ladies met in pubs and public transport), as he was Hollywood stars and starlets. By one biographer's estimate, Burton must have made a conquest of over 2,000 women during the height of his fame and virility – including women whose names he might not have known. Of his more famous alleged romantic interests while married to Sybil were:

- *The Robe* (1953) co-star, **Jean Simmons** (wife of actor Stewart Granger), whom he reportedly took great lengths to arrange to see in secret even while they he *and* Sybil were guests in the home of Jean *and* her husband;
- *Rains of Ranchipur* (1955) co-star, **Lana Turner** is said to have counted him among *her* many conquests as Hollywood's "love goddess;"
- His frequent **co-star Claire Bloom** (in the films *Alexander the Great*, *Look Back in*

Anger, The Spy Who Came in from the Cold, and on the stage with *The Lady's Not for Burning* and *Hamlet*), with whom he would have an on-off affair for five years. She found him hypnotic and wonderful, but also felt he was engaged in affairs with other women. This was proven when she reportedly caught him kissing American actress Susan Strasberg, which ended whatever she had with Burton sometime around 1958;

- **Susan Strasberg** was the daughter of famed Method proponent, Lee Strasberg, and Marilyn Monroe's infamous coach, Paula. Susan was a beautiful girl with plenty of prospects, starting out young in the entertainment industry via modeling, television, film and stage. It was on the last that she would fall head over heels for an opportunistic Richard Burton (it was said he wasn't really in love with her). They worked together in New York for *Time Remembered* (1957), where, she would reportedly say, *"he laid his passion at my feet…"* She was a 19-year-old stunner, and the co-stars reportedly acted on their desires during *Time Remembered's* run. She is said to have visited him while he was working on *Look Back in Anger*, which was when they may have been caught together by Claire Bloom… at a time when he was also alleged to have been sleeping with co-star, **Mary Ure**;

- A then-underage **Rosemary Kingsland** who would later write about the affair she had with Burton while she was a schoolgirl and he, a theater star twice her age. She would provide exquisite detail on the romance, but give little hard evidence to convince her skeptics; and

- A range of other women were linked to Burton to varying degrees, including co-stars Angie Dickinson and Barbara Rush and, fantastically, the 20 girls on the chorus line of *Camelot*, if legend holds true.

The long-suffering Sybil is said to have survived by regarding her husband's entanglements as rumors or overinflated flirtations. When *Cleopatra* came around and her husband's affair with Elizabeth Taylor became hot property on the press, however, there was no more turning away. She filed for a divorce, reportedly citing "*abandonment and cruel and inhumane treatment.*" She was awarded custody of their two children and a million-dollar settlement, which was quite the sum at the time.

Life after being Mrs. Burton included opening a nightclub in New York in partnership with friends in the entertainment industry, including Julie Andrews and Stephen Sondheim. Arthur, as the club was called, became a hotspot for years, with icons of the era - Truman Capote, Andy Warhol, Tennessee Williams and Wilt Chamberlain among them - walking through its doors. She married singer Jordan Christopher, who led Arthur's house band, in 1966 and they would be married until he died in 1996. Sybil eventually sold the hotspot and focused on other successful endeavors, such as the New Theater in Manhattan and the Bay Street Theatre in Sag

Harbor. She passed away in 2013 at the age of 83.

Elizabeth Taylor

Elizabeth Taylor was the consummate star. The actress was born beautiful, with a rare violet eye color to cap her already-stunning features. She started performing at age 3, did film work a few years later and met with early and sustained stardom; she therefore knew no other life. Her debut was with *One Born Every Minute* (1942) – she was 10 years old. After *National Velvet* (1944), she was a star at aged 12. She continued to work in Hollywood, and grew up dazzling audiences with her unwavering loveliness and, as she got older, a show-stopping figure to match. There was no awkward stage for this legendary beauty.

She was known for her looks but also for being constantly in love – and when in love, she tended to get married. She started early and a good thing perhaps, for she would have eight marriages with seven men over her lifetime. Husband number one was hotel heir, Nicky Hilton, whom she wed in 1950 when she was barely out of her teens. Shortly after that, she wed the much older British actor, Michael Wilding in 1952. They would have two sons together. Husband number three was the influential producer Mike Todd, a man of outside personality who liked showering his wife with outrageous presents. They had one child, a daughter, before he died in a plane crash. The widow would be swept up by a friend of Todd's, singer and actor, Eddie Fisher – who was married to America's sweetheart,

Debbie Reynolds. Taylor landed the label of a homewrecker, but she and Fisher wed in 1959.

And then came Richard Burton, who in 1964 became husband number five. They divorced for a short time and re-married in 1975, thus making Burton, also husband number six. The reunion wouldn't last long, and Taylor would go on to wed Senator John Warner in 1976. Being a politician's wife did not suit either, and so out went husband number seven and last came number eight, the surprising, low-key construction worker, Larry Fortensky in 1991 whom she would also divorce in 1996.

Of eight marriages with seven husbands, Elizabeth Taylor regarded Richard Burton as her great love; she had, after all, married him twice. It has even been said that he wrote her a last love letter shortly before he died, one that she treasured and kept close, one that spoke of yearning to return to her, one that she would request to be buried in.

Their union was so larger-than-life that "Taylor & Burton," or "Liz & Dick" as they would often be referred to, can only be approximated by characters of fiction in some of the greatest love stories that the world had ever read - like Heathcliff and Cathy; or Romeo and Juliet; and maybe even, Anthony and Cleopatra…

The "Liz & Dick" Show

In many ways, the scandalous affair between Elizabeth Taylor and her co-star Richard Burton during the filming of *Cleopatra*, was just one more headache in a litany of pains suffered by the production. But first, some context. The 1960s was time of social change in the United States, and Hollywood was no exception, suffering its own set of growing pains.

Television ownership was up, suburban living on the rise and broadcast coverage wider. All these meant that cinema-going audiences were on the decline, what with all the bother it took to go to the movies downtown, while free options were available right in the living room. The studio system was also on the decline; a key decision by the Supreme Court lessened their powers of distributing content to their own theaters. Another impactful decision dealt a blow to the censorship code followed by the film industry at the time; movies were decided to be forms of artistic expression and therefore, covered as freedom of speech. What this ultimately meant was that (1) less ticket sales meant less funds going to the studios; (2) studios now had to be more selective in the movies they made, not only because they had fewer funds to go around but also because they couldn't just force theaters they once owned to show whatever they had created; and (3) the studios had competition not only from television, but also from foreign films that could now be selected by more independent theaters, and/or be more compelling to audiences because they were made without the restriction of the codes Hollywood had long been more or less following. Aside from these financial and legal issues, fears of communism had given rise to blacklists in Hollywood that either ended careers of talented figures, or driven them away to work in other countries to do projects that could eventually make its way to America anyway.

The result of these changes meant some of the smallest number of film outputs by Hollywood since its history. Studios bucked and fought against the tide of course, ushering in innovations to court audiences back into the theaters – filming more movies in color (which was still an issue for television); widescreen projections; 3-D; and of course, the rise of the epic movie – a spectacle that needed a theater for full appreciation of its big stories, long running times, sweeping settings, and casts of thousands. Sometimes they worked and other times, they did not. The "epic movie" at the time, was akin to placing all of one's eggs in one basket. It was a large gamble that sometimes did not pay off. Many studios ended up folding during this turbulent time, and the outfit behind the epic movie *Cleopatra*, 20th Century Fox, almost suffered the same fate after the movie's disappointing performance.

Cleopatra was originally conceived as a more straightforward, $2 million movie. Film producer Walter Wanger, however, sold the studio on a grander vision, which also eventually included the casting of Elizabeth Taylor in the title role. Her casting wasn't an immediate thrill for studio heads, but she was at least expected to bring in box office numbers. Courting the actress into the project began in 1959, and came with a hefty price tag. She was a $1 million talent, with a sure salary plus payment contingent on time the production extended, plus a share of the gross. She also had a generous living allowance. She came on board with an unprecedented deal that floored everyone in Tinsel Town, but that wouldn't even be the end of it. A complex, disorganized and some say cursed production ended up giving her a payout several times larger than that, on top of the film's other financial woes.

To begin with, the script was in shambles, having gone through a number of writers and re-do's. Shooting thus began without a final script, which meant no proper production plan, which in turn led to waste of time and film. The original shooting site in England also proved to be a mistake, with technical limitations that did not accommodate the set design and filming demands of an epic movie, as well as tough unions. The English weather proved to be a challenge too, especially when it harmed the health of the leading lady. The director, Rouben Mamoulian was not in full control. The delays kept on coming. The budget kept swelling.

Director Joseph L. Mankiewicz was brought in, but also at a cost; the studios reportedly had to buy him out of his previous commitments. His entrance brought massive changes to the angle of the story and so, a new script to go with it. Though there was cause to hope the changes would improve the production, the leading lady suddenly fell ill again, and much worse this time. A severe sickness brought hear near death, and required her to have an emergency tracheotomy. She rallied, but needed months to recover.

When filming resumed, the production had a new home in Italy. But still without a finalized script, work on it was expensive and inefficient. Film, money and time were all wasted by lack of production planning, which had little more than an outline to work from.

Then came "*Le Scandale.*"

The changes over the course of the production eventually brought in a re-cast Caesar (played by Rex Harrison), and a re-cast Mark Anthony (played by Richard Burton). Burton was fresh off of his Tony victory for *Camelot* on Broadway. *Cleopatra* was going to be his biggest film.

It wasn't love at first sight between the couple who would forever after be known as "Liz & Dick," but he, like pretty much every male to come before him, found her extraordinarily beautiful. Unlike other men though, Richard Burton found words to describe her – *"famine, fire, destruction and plague…"*

Beauty aside, he reportedly did not think much of her as an actress. She in turn was aware of – and unimpressed by – his reputation as a gifted actor but a hard-living, womanizing Welshman. They came from drastically different worlds too; he had a hardscrabble background, while she was a pampered and privileged girl who quickly became a star and stayed that way for all of her life. But they found things in common; they were both bold, courageous personalities with irreverent humor.

They did not meet on the set of *Cleopatra*. That distinction went to a party long before filming, and she had decided to ignore him, as he was an incessant talker whom she found "*rather full of himself.*" But fate brought them together for *Cleopatra*. She had no plans of falling for the actor, who had a reputation for romancing his co-stars, but one particular incident reportedly softened her heart.

He was on set and hungover. His hands shook so badly he couldn't even drink a cup of coffee. The leading lady reportedly swept in for the rescue, helping him bring the beverage to his mouth. She found his sweet vulnerability humanizing, and the incident endeared her to him.

Later, they would be more open about their admiration of each other. She found him "*magnificent.*" He called her body 'a work of genius' and 'a miracle of construction.' Her breasts, he would call "*apocalyptic.*" But he would tease and be critical of her looks on occasion too, citing her double chin and short legs. Whether or not he meant it though, Richard Burton was plain ensnared by the Hollywood diva's beauty early on in their working relationship, and they had great sexual chemistry and energy.

Both Taylor and Burton were married to other people when they started *Cleopatra* (and on each other). He, to first wife Sybil Williams and she, to Eddie Fisher, who was her fourth husband. Their secret relationship wouldn't be one for very long, though. Those on set felt their palpable connection. By the time their first on-screen kiss came around, they did it longer than was necessary. Soon, there was love to be made wherever they found opportunity.

Elizabeth Taylor's image had already taken a hit after she snagged Fisher from the famous sweetheart, Debbie Reynolds, and sneaking around with an also-married Burton did not help her rebuild public trust at all once the affair was revealed. The pair received ire from many quarters. They were regarded as poor examples to the youth and a menace against the sanctity of marriage. Even some of their friends could not stand what they were doing.

Sybil, for example, reportedly cut off speaking with Burton for good. He continued to support her and their children though, as he would continue to support many people over the course of his career (he was known to be generous even to hangers-on). His relationship with mentor, Philip Burton, also took a hit and they would be at odds supposedly for years. Nevertheless the affair consumed Burton and Taylor both. Not even a strongly-worded and very public disapproval by the Vatican could deter them from their passion for each other. It was the biggest scandal of its day, and everyone was attuned to everything the pair was up to and they were up to *a lot*.

In the meantime, *Cleopatra* wrapped and spiraled toward financial trouble. By the time they wrapped, the production had spent $30 million, and spent an additional $15 million on promotion. In today's money, the total spent on *Cleopatra* is in the hundreds of millions. Reviews were rather dismal, but at least Taylor and Burton drew curious crowds into the theaters; it was the highest grosser of 1963 – though it still wouldn't be enough to cover what was spent in making it. The film would be out of the red only years later, when television paid big money to air it. It did, however, bring home four Oscars for Art Direction, Cinematography, Costume Design and Visual Effects.

Taylor and Burton divorced their spouses and married in 1964. They stayed together for ten years, living large before the eyes of the world. They were busy working actors and jet-setters dragging around their children and a large entourage, and they paid for the best everywhere their traveling circus went.

They loved each other openly, spent with little regard for caution, fought and made up with abandon. They liked parties and drinking. They lived lavishly, from hotel suites and the yacht, *Kalizma*, with their fancy cars, paintings by the Masters and owning multiple luxury properties all over the world. They were generous to each other, too. A grand symbol of the excesses of their union is the 69.42-carat, pear-shaped Taylor-Burton Diamond, which was reportedly once given by the Indian emperor of Taj Mahal-fame, to his bride.

Over the course of their first marriage, they made many films together. Most were forgettable, but *Who's Afraid of Virginia Woolf?* Became a classic and won for Taylor her second Oscar; and *The Taming of the Shrew* was well received.

But it was a financially, physically and mentally draining relationship. One could only love, fight, make-up, drink, party and spend so much without tiring. They had intense feelings for each other, yes – she dealt with his vices, and he would write to her often, even when they were in the same place and she was only a room away - but it soon became clear that strong passions were not enough to sustain a successful marriage. He was said to have continued drinking and became increasingly dissatisfied with the mediocre roles he's had to perform just to keep up with financial obligations. The vulnerability he felt made him an even easier target for women – "*I flatter and am flattered and both too easily*," he had once written to his then-wife – and reportedly returned to his womanizing. The once flirty, passionate fights became more real and more embittered. And, gifted as he was with words, Richard Burton had the ability to be scathing. He was also hurting from the death of his brother and constant companion, Ifor. It brought him to drink more, and he became even more unimpressed with his life.

Divorce came in 1974, with Elizabeth stating their differences were too marked and she had tried everything she could. Less than a year later though, in the middle of settling affairs relating to divorce, a moving reunion had them back in each other's arms and back into Marriage, Take Two. Except, nothing had really changed. There was love as there always had been, but Burton was still Burton, and he wasn't easy. Neither was the Hollywood diva, whose history of ailments eventually found her increasingly needy, and reliant on painkillers to boot. Their second marriage crumbled quickly, in spite of all the hopes a reunion inspired. Burton's romance with a free-spirited blonde model drastically different from his wife, and Taylor's own lonely transgressions with other men put an abrupt end to the heartfelt, well-intentioned reunion.

"I know the best is yet to be," she had written him with hope and romance shortly after they were reunited. But it was not. Burton reportedly asked for a divorce and he got it. Their second marriage ended in 1976 and shortly afterwards, Burton married model Suzy Hunt while Elizabeth Taylor eventually found romance and her own succeeding marriage with Senator John Warner. They would marry other people after these marriages, too.

Encounters after 1976 – especially during the run of the Noel Coward play, *Private Lives* wherein they both starred - would still show their spark and fuel rumors of a Taylor-Burton Take Three, but it would never be again. Burton married his final wife, Sally

Hay, on a break from the play in 1983. By 1984, he was dead of cerebral hemorrhage at the age of 58.

Burton had once said that his union with Elizabeth was *"a rough old ride, but I wouldn't swap travelling with Elizabeth for anything on earth."* He had uttered these words in the early 1970s. In another interview after their second marriage, he had been quoted as saying, *"…it didn't work out this time – maybe it will next time…"* It is lines like these – plus the revelation of his Elizabeth Taylor-dominated diaries years later - that continues to fuel talk that they were each other's greatest love, and that he might have even wanted to return to Taylor towards the end of his life. This was a claim that obviously displeased the woman who became his final wife, Sally Hay.

Hay would even contest the existence of the so-called 'last love letter' Burton is said to have written his two-time ex-wife shortly before his death. This treasured and mysterious letter, which went publicly unseen, is rumored to indicate some desire on the part of Burton to return "home" to Elizabeth Taylor. There would even be reports of the Hollywood diva being buried with it. But Hay had a good relationship with Burton, and his writings, later to be revealed in the excellently written, insightful *The Richard Burton Diaries*, would reveal he had frustrations with "ET" while they were working on *Private Lives* on the stage together. Perhaps sadder than fiery frustration, however, was that he seemed to have ceased to be bewitched by her, with one entry speaking of how he felt sorry for her situation, "*A mass of a mess.*" One searing entry even went on to say "ET" was "*beginning to bore,*" a phenomenon he once thought impossible. "*How terrible a thing time is.*"

Hay also reportedly claimed that Burton couldn't have written the 'last love letter' at the time, because he was very ill and she was nursing him. Lawyers she is said to have consulted with were also unaware of any such letter being written for Taylor. Still, the existence of a final letter made for a great story – and it certainly fed 'the greatest love affair' narrative of Taylor and Burton that remains too romantic to simply let die.

Susan Hunt

But before Sally Hay, there was beautiful and popular British model, Suzy Miller.

According to one biographer, Burton saw Suzy – then the wife of champion British race car driver, James Hunt – on the slopes in Switzerland in December, 1975 while he was still married to Elizabeth Taylor. The tall blonde caught the eye right away, and Burton was smitten. She was, at 26 years old, 22 years younger than him. They thereafter ran into each other at a party and began a friendship, which quickly intensified into romance, even as they were both married to other people.

If accounts hold true, Burton paid $1 million to be able to quickly extricate Suzy from her famous race car driving husband, who also had a wandering eye. Some had looked upon the arrangement between James Hunt and Richard Burton with disdain, because from a certain perspective, Suzy Hunt was "*traded*" or "*sold.*" Steep as the price tag was though, the marriage only lasted for six years. Hunt and Burton were separated before they divorced in 1976, around the time Richard Burton was working on the TV mini-series, *Wagner*. Suzy, however, is said to have helped him decrease his drinking.

Sally Hay

Richard Burton met his last wife, Sally Hay, while filming *Wagner*, where he starred and she was a production assistant. When they wed in 1983, he was in his late-50's and she, in her mid-30's. Their marriage did not last long, cut short when he died by age 58. But Burton made a lasting impact on his much younger, final wife, and she was so confident in their union that she had even allowed her husband's Elizabeth Taylor-filled writing to be published in the 2000's. Burton had apparently started writing at 14 and continued to do so almost right up to his death. There were some gaps in between, but the writing was heaviest when he had been with Taylor.

Sally recognized that her husband and the late Hollywood diva had an impassioned romance, but it sometimes frustrated her that the duo were packaged as the great love affair that could have reunited toward the end of his life, when Burton already had a life with *her*. And it was a quiet life; Sally would speak of how she did his make-up, and watched *Private Lives* starring Taylor and Burton from the wings or listened to it from a speaker backstage, then they would have supper at home together. It was a life that reportedly brought Burton calm contentment until he died. Indeed, of Sally, he had reportedly once told a confidante, "*Thank God I've found her.*"

Sally never remarried, and is instrumental in keeping Richard Burton's legacy alive. She runs philanthropic activities under his name for writing and drama, and allowed the publishing of his writings too, via *The Richard Burton Diaries*.

If Only

The Richard Burton Diaries was a project Sally Hay was enthusiastic about, especially given her late husband's passion for the written word. She gave content to the University of Wales in 2005; it was edited by Professor Chris Williams of the University of Wales at Swansea, which would receive part of the proceeds. Burton's daughter, the actress Kate, reportedly read the proofs while Burton's stepson with Elizabeth Taylor, Christopher Wilding, shared entries by his mother. Sally welcomed the opportunity for people "*to see the world through his eyes.*"

And those stunning eyes had seen much.

He was a Welsh boy who had done well for himself, the coal miner's son who held and owned and given away the world's finest diamonds, who would marry twice one of the most beautiful women to ever walk the planet. He stood admired before crowds and cameras, but also had stood in their disapproval and judgment. He'd had acclaim but also poor reviews. He'd played great roles and mediocre ones. He'd known crazy love and quiet contentment. It was a life cut short, but made rich by his experiences, which he faced with intelligence and humor, and that few people could have worded as well as he did in his writings.

Great memories of Richard Burton's talent, as was mentioned earlier in this book, is always followed by the word "but." A gifted actor, but he had a tumultuous personal life. An intelligent and passionate man, but he had his demons. What is more tragic, however, is when these contradictions are followed by the longing of "If Only."

He was just 58 when he died, of cerebral hemorrhage in Switzerland. He fell ill one morning while in his villa in Celigny outside Geneva, and was taken to a hospital where he later died. His loving wife Sally was with him. He'd long been in poor health – a near-lifetime of smoking and alcohol was going to take its toll eventually - but the death was sudden because they came from a recent holiday, he was in fine spirits and was looking well. He had several projects on the horizon too.

Richard Burton is the most nominated actor to never win an Oscar. He died relatively young, and was still working at the time. Who knows what more he would have made of more years?

Indeed, he was so much more than the drinking and the women and The Woman who dominated the public narrative of his life. He was so much more. But what perhaps hurts the most is that he could have been even greater. He is often remembered in terms of lost promise, and with this lost promise, is a bittersweet legacy of fine performances, weighed by thoughts of what could have been.

Elizabeth Taylor

An Elizabeth Taylor Biography

Katy Holborn

Table of Contents

Elizabeth Taylor – The Last Legend of Hollywood

Introduction

The Golden Age of Hollywood

The Queen of Hollywood

The Road to Stardom
Elizabeth Taylor-Hilton-Wilding-Todd-Fisher-Burton-Burton-Warner-Fortensky

Mrs. Hilton (1950)

Mrs. Wilding (1952)

Mrs. Todd (1957)

Mrs. Fisher (1959)

Mrs. Burton (1964-1974); (1975 -1976)

Mrs. Warner (1976)

Mrs. Fortensky (1991)

Legacy of a Survivor

Elizabeth Taylor's Goodbye

An Ever Shining Star

Elizabeth Taylor – The Last Legend of Hollywood

Introduction

"Movie Star."

The term conjures up images of limousines and red carpets, of camera flashes bouncing light against the facets of brilliant diamonds softened only by thick, pristine white fur, wound around the elegant, beautiful bodies of larger-than-life, outsize personalities. Sometimes they have in hand golden statuettes symbolizing their place at the top, held like the scepter of a queen, or the spear of a victorious warrior. These stars can have mercurial personalities – when they smile they sparkle, when they are angry they burn. When they fall in love, it seems as if they magnetize madly only toward each other. These are celestial, almost alien beings – far removed from the common people's daily lives.

Chances are, if you ever wanted to be an actor, this is what you had in mind. The traditional Hollywood fantasy isn't about a star photographed without makeup doing normal, everyday things like wearing leggings and fluffy boots while lined up for security screening at the airport, or clad in a track suit on the way to the gym. The traditional fantasy isn't about red carpets where young starlets eschew high heels and young men arrive without ties. The traditional fantasy isn't about stars riding on the subway, or doing things like pumping gas, shopping at the grocery, or picking up after their dogs. Old time celebrity was unabashed in its glamor, unafraid and unashamed to say – no, we are not just like you.

Chief amongst these most distant of celestial bodies is Dame Elizabeth Taylor, among the last – if not *the* last – legend to come out of the Golden Age of Hollywood. For most of her life, she was chief transmitter of Tinsel Town's illusion and fantasy. She was "Movie Star" par excellence. Not just by acting chops, though these she had – two Academy Awards can vouch for that – but by her unabashed epitomizing of Hollywood glamour. She had no pretensions to being anything other than the rare creature that she was born to be. Love her or hate her, Liz was Liz.

In a world of 'go big or go home,' Elizabeth Taylor never *ever* went home. In an industry which called for beauty, hers was a perfectly symmetrical face with the rare, blazing violet eyes. When she fell in love, she married. When she married, she married eight times. When she had a very public, high profile love affair, it was condemned by the Vatican. When she went out, she dressed to the nines and appeared in stunning diamonds. When she made a flop like *Cleopatra* (1963), the scale of its failings was so epic it became a cautionary tale. When she worked, she worked seemingly forever; her storied career stretched for almost 70 years. When she made friends, she fought for them tirelessly – her famous devotion to the AIDS cause was due to her deep friendship with the actor, Rock Hudson, who had suffered from it. She was a mother figure to eccentric music great, the late Michael Jackson too; she gave him his first Christmas, spent afternoons watching Disney movies with him, and staunchly stood by him when he was accused of improper behavior against minors. She was just as devoted to stunning actor, Montgomery Clift, with whom she starred in several films. When he had a car crash, she was amongst the first on the scene and she pulled dislodged teeth from inside his mouth to keep him from choking.

These are just a few of the legends around Elizabeth Taylor. A story that would otherwise seem fantastic on any other actress, has the patina of possibility with her. Because even in a land that peddled make-believe, she was sometimes strange and otherworldly. She sparkled even among stars.

The Golden Age of Hollywood

We can thank "The Golden Age of Hollywood" for the illusion of the "Movie Star." The period is commonly believed to have started in the late 1920's, most marked by the release of *The Jazz Singer* (1927). Though hardly the first talking picture it is sometimes perceived to be, the film popularized talkies and proved they were technologically feasible and financially viable. Soon, the last of the silent movies would be made and give way to the exciting new possibilities of movies with dialogue and music.

The heady period of filmmaking from the 1930s to the 1950s can be attributed to several factors. First, there were so many new ideas that new technologies especially in sound, allowed to prosper. Second, the movies had a virtual monopoly on entertainment mass media. No television, no home video, no internet – meant no competition. The movies were practically uncontested, and the industry could churn out a lot of output and expect film-going audiences to pay at least some attention. Movies even continued to be made during the crippling financial crisis of the Great Depression. If anything, it actually drew audiences into theaters as a means of escaping their troubles. Even World War II was not a deterrent; if anything, the movies became a tool for propaganda and a way of lifting morale.

Moreover, the period was marked by unparalleled control of all this uncontested audience by a few big studios – they had a hand in making and keeping stars and in making and distributing movies. The largest studios even had their own chain of theaters to screen their films. At the time, "The Big 5" were 20th Century Fox, Metro-Goldwyn-Mayer, Paramount, RKO and Warner Brothers.

This meant fierce rivalries, and competition that could elevate the quality of output. The studio system also meant that all the financial boon of a growth in movies would go to just a few players, so these few players had financial elbow room to either take risks and be more experimental with films, or simply just churn out a lot of output, or both. The money was flowing, and film budgets reflected that. Furthermore, because the studios were so powerful, they had a firm control on their contract artists' lives; which meant keeping the artists on script in real life aside from their reel life, so that the actors and actresses could continue to maintain and cultivate the love, attention and box office receipts of their devoted fanbases, without deviation from their public image.

These intoxicating years ushered in some of the greatest films of all time; not just during their period, but to be viewed and treasured by generations to come after it. Among them were *Gone With The Wind* (1939), *The Wizard of Oz* (1939), *Rebecca* (1940), *Citizen Kane* (1941), *Casablanca* (1942), *It's A Wonderful Life* (1946), *All About Eve* (1950), *Sunset Blvd* (1950), *Singin' in the Rain* (1952), *Rear Window*, (1954), *Ben-Hur* (1959), *Some Like it*

Hot (1959) and *Psycho* (1960) – just to name a few! Here were epics, romances, comedies, social films, musicals, suspense – it seemed there was greatness to be found in any genre.

But as they say, all good things must come to an end, and many factors contributed to the closing of this golden period in filmmaking.

Television took a chunk out of the film-going audience, though did not kill it altogether, as some early pundits feared. The proposition television offered was an irresistible one; cheap entertainment from the comfort on your own home. It also prospered because of the rise in suburban living, where cinemas downtown necessitated extra effort just to get to for a movie. Filmmakers bucked and fought against the threat, ushering in innovations like beautiful color, and enhancements on the theater experience such as 3-D viewing, widescreen, surround sound, and the production of the Epic Movie genre that demanded a large screen to be fully enjoyed. Still, they bled out audiences once television became truly national at around 1948; if the late 40s saw almost 100 million Americans going to the movies weekly, by the early 1950s, there would be half of that. Movies managed to weather the storm and endure, but now had clear competition.

Aside from television, the movie industry also had to deal with government antitrust regulations. A lot of the studios' previously uncontested powers eroded, and soon they had to be more selective of what they spent their budgets on. There were larger bets on safer choices, and so, fewer movies.

Sometimes though, even these "safe" choices did not work out and with so much at stake on a single project, it could lead to disastrous financial effects.

Studios also lost much of their control over their actors. Large stars eventually found their voice to buck against ill-fitting roles, undesirable projects, or their contracts altogether. They had greater powers to assert some control over their creative lives. New stars would follow suit. The converse of this though, is that while talent now had more freedom, they also had fewer protections from all-powerful studios who once could have shielded them from scandal. Tabloid and gossip media culture rose around this time too, with little studios could do to control the bad press around the occasional indiscretions of a star. Tabloid culture demystified them, and also sometimes brought about ruin for the prospects of an actor.

Politics would also play a role in curbing the creative energy of this era. In the years after World War II, fears of Communism would blacklist and silence visionary voices if they were perceived as sympathetic to Soviet or leftist causes. These included actors, writers and directors and other creative minds. It's not only those who were blacklisted that were affected; everyone else also had to tread with caution.

Of course there were upsides to the factors that ended Hollywood's Golden Age. Eventually, there would be a place for both small and silver screen in the entertainment industry and quality would be churned out from both movies and television. The decrease in the powers of the studios democratized filmmaking, ushering in fresh new voices that took on the mantle of courage and experimentation. It also democratized film viewing, giving audiences a wide variety of film genres and styles to see and choose from. Stars found their own creative agency and could be more daring in their roles, to challenge themselves and to deviate from typecasting. They could also free or spare themselves from restrictive agreements, as well as pursue better entitlements in their contracts. Some of those who worked behind the scenes, like writers, directors and producers, would also benefit from similar freedoms.

From a combination of these and other factors, it is widely believed that by the early

1960s, the Golden Age of Hollywood has come to an end. And ever afterwards, even as we can acknowledge the positive effects to come from its conclusion, we still cannot help but long for the gilded Hollywood image we were presented from its Golden Age. It was, as many an expert had remarked, one of the greatest concentration of creative talents to ever be in the same place at the same time.

The era has since become romanticized and enlarged to mythic proportions. In this way, the Golden of Age of Hollywood is like Atlantis or Camelot - a time and place where legends are born. Here, perched between myth and reality, between what we can know for a fact and what we long to know, is where magnificent personalities reside.

And amongst the most unforgettable of these creatures is Elizabeth Taylor.

The Queen of Hollywood

Elizabeth Taylor was a Golden Age actress, a "real" Movie Star, perhaps even "the last" such "real" Movie Star when she passed away in 2011. She was undoubtedly of the era, having worked in the entertainment industry from the time she was 9 years old in 1942 (for *There's One Born Every Minute*), through the end of the Golden Age in the late 1950s (and well afterwards until the early 2000s)… Except, interestingly, the most immediately memorable outputs of the Golden Age of Hollywood did not feature a singularly iconic moment for her.

Of her legendary peers, consider: blonde bombshell, Marilyn Monroe (born in 1926), made movie magic singing *"Diamonds are a girl's best friend…"* in *Gentlemen Prefer Blondes* (1953), and sent many hearts aflutter when her frilly white dress was kicked up by a subway breeze in *The Seven Year Itch* (1955). Hollywood Ice Queen and suspense master Alfred Hitchcock's muse, Grace Kelly (born in 1929), had one of the greatest character entrances in movie history in *Rear Window*. Gamine ingénue, Audrey Hepburn (born in 1929), wowed in Givenchy and fulfilled our Cinderella fantasies in *Sabrina* (1954). If anything, the most iconic and widely-used image of Elizabeth Taylor in character was when she played the title role in *Cleopatra* – which was one of the greatest critical and commercial disappointments of all time when it came out, overblown and over-budget in 1963.

This is not a slander on her career, for it was a good one, and a long one. It just seems as if, for all its good and bad, her star sometimes outshone the characters she played, and her movies. Her star might even be accused of outshining her own performances, such that it can be taken for granted just how good of an actress she really was. And she could be fantastic; two Academy Award wins could attest to that, for *BUtterfield 8* (1960) and *Who's Afraid of Virginia Woolf?* (1966). She was even nominated four times in a row from 1957 to 1960, for *Raintree County* (1957), *Cat on a Hot Tin Roof* (1958), *Suddenly, Last Summer* (1959), and *BUtterfield 8*, when she finally won. But her star power can be overwhelming. Of her breakthrough performance in *National Velvet* (1944), critic James Agee found her beautiful and wonderful, and reportedly stated, "*I hardly know or care whether she can act or not...*" The question of her acting prowess would remain up until the new millennium – as Tom Dewe Mathews of *The Guardian* opined – "*She wasn't much of an actress, but...*" And indeed, it is the "but" that is unquestionable even for detractors of her talent – *but* she was magnificent to look at, not just for her looks but for her glorious presence. She was such a scene-stealer.

The type of legacy she left behind may have also been affected by timing. She was reared on the Golden Age, but her ascendency to leading lady status came when the old system was in decline and its positive effects still nascent. Her *Cleopatra* misadventure may have even been symptomatic of that, as it was made and released at an intersection of the effects of the end of the Golden Age – it was a gigantic gamble on a genre that should have been a cinematic draw, but did not pay off. It probably did not help that tabloid culture was also on the rise, and her forbidden romance with co-star Richard Burton gave them fodder for months.

Perhaps it is also hard to associate Elizabeth Taylor with a single iconic image (save for the infamous *Cleopatra*) because of her longevity, which is notable amongst her fellow screen goddesses. Marilyn Monroe's filmography spanned 29 movies over 16 years before her untimely death at the age of 36. Grace Kelly barely had a dozen films over six years before she stepped away from Hollywood to become the Princess of Monaco in 1956 – she was 27. Audrey Hepburn was really only active for a decade or so too, doing major roles in just a little over a dozen films between 1951 to 1967.

Elizabeth Taylor, on the other hand, had been around for so long, in so many memorable incarnations. Was she, for example to be remembered as the fresh-faced Velvet Brown in her star-making, *National Velvet* (1944)? Was she the emerging, lovely leading lady in *A Place in the Sun* (1951)? Was she the passionate, spirited Maggie the Cat of *Cat on a Hot Tin Roof* (1958)? The promiscuous Gloria Wandrous of *BUtterfield 8*? Was she Cleopatra incarnate or the domineering, embittered Martha of *Who's Afraid of Virginia Woolf?* Was she the Elizabeth Taylor remembered by younger generations for her perfume ads? Was she even the glamorous, eccentric "Elizabeth Taylor" she played in several television shows of the 1990's that have cast her to play *herself*?

In the family sitcom, *The Nanny*, she asked the titular nanny, Fran (played by comic actress, Fran Drescher) if she had ever been married. Fran replied no, and "Elizabeth Taylor" asked, with a winsome, wide-eyed, gentle disbelief: "*Not even once?*"

Fran then admitted, she had come close once, "*But then I thought about it…*" Elizabeth Taylor thereafter gave out a throaty laugh, and with a dismissive wave of a graceful hand she declared, "*That was your mistake, dear.*"

This and other audience-pleasing cameos playing herself, were amongst the last of Elizabeth Taylor's work in the entertainment industry, and it shows us several things about Elizabeth Taylor's place in Hollywood's legendarium.

First, her "Elizabeth Taylor" persona had somehow become a fleshed-out, distinct character who could actually be played.

Second, this "Elizabeth Taylor" character was an agglomeration of her professional self and her personal self; of her public self and her private self. It is difficult to compartmentalize her life, and parcel out where one begins and one ends. Reel and real had become entangled.

Not to say that the depiction is accurate; she herself was aware of this *"public me… the one named Elizabeth Taylor…"* but she found it largely untrue and as a matter of fact, *"slightly revolting."* But the public could only know and assemble what we perceive, and indeed, as director Joseph L. Mankiewicz (who had worked with her on *Suddenly, Last Summer* and *Cleopatra*) once reportedly said, for Elizabeth Taylor, living was akin to acting. So if we looked at her life as an act, and her acts as showing parts of her life and herself… could we not also look at her sometimes as if she was a character?

Finally, whoever this "Elizabeth Taylor" character was, she had become a fixture in pop culture. She had been a part of the industry for so long – almost seven decades! – that she was practically synonymous with glamor and Hollywood. She never knew another life, and Hollywood as we now know and understand it, spent much of its history having her in it. One was almost unimaginable without the other.

Elizabeth Taylor was the last of the Golden Age actresses by the 2000s, but she was also a movie star, a TV star, a tabloid mainstay, and a pioneer in celebrity advertisements and product branding. She managed to be a celebrity, no matter the entertainment era she was in. She lived in the Golden Age yes, but she brought the gild everywhere, every time. She was both an artistic talent and a bankable, commercial star. She had art, but she also had salesmanship.

Elizabeth Taylor, in short, wasn't just the Queen of Hollywood - she was Hollywood. When she passed away in 2011, she left the world not with a costumed, iconic image – she left us with a brand.

The Road to Stardom

For Elizabeth Taylor, the road to stardom would be short and on the express lane.

Elizabeth Rosemond Taylor was born in London on the 27th of February, 1932. She was born in England but her parents, Sara Viola Warmbrodt and Francis Lenn Taylor, were both Americans. The Taylors were art dealers. Sara, however, had been on the New York stage as actress "Sara Sothern" before getting married; in this way, perhaps Elizabeth had performing in her blood. She certainly manifested an early interest and aptitude for it, taking up singing and dancing at age three (two years old, according to some accounts!), and reportedly even having a recital before the royal family including the Princesses Elizabeth and Margaret. It was also at around this age that she picked up horseback riding, which would be useful to her career later.

The Taylor family – Sara, Francis, Elizabeth and her older brother, Howard – would live in London until the threat of war in 1939 prompted them to leave Europe for the safety of the United States. They settled in Los Angeles, where Elizabeth's striking good looks would be drawn into the Hollywood machine before long. There seemed no fate more fitting to someone of such rare beauty; her violet eyes were a rarity and the double row of lashes that surrounded them were literally from a genetic mutation.

With encouragement and / or pressure from her ambitious mother, Elizabeth pursued an acting career. Sara Taylor would be a constant force behind and beside her for her early professional life, sometimes allegedly pushing her to her very limits.

Not long after the family's move, Elizabeth did a screen test for Universal Studios and landed her first film. She was only 9 years old on the set of *There's One Born Every Minute* (1942). She starred with Carl Switzer of *Our Gang*'s Alfalfa-fame, but she didn't quite set the right impression for the studio and would be dropped after the one project. The family was friends with an MGM producer named Sam Marx though, and he would help her get a screen test for the upcoming *Lassie Comes Home* (1943). She landed the part and afterwards, a contract that would allow her to pursue a succession of other projects. Most of her most important film work would eventually be with MGM.

It was *National Velvet* (1944) that turned her into a star. The film adaptation of the novel by Enid Bagnold called for a horseback-riding child actress with a decent English accent, and 12-year-old Elizabeth Taylor was pretty much an ideal fit – except for her height. She needed to be taller. And so, one of the earliest, slightly strange, almost unreal Elizabeth Taylor stories started going around; that she had literally stretched herself to fit the requirements of the role.

If she really did it, the work certainly paid off. Not only did she get the part of Velvet Brown, but the movie (which top-billed established actor, Mickey Rooney), was a big hit with critics and audiences alike. *National*

Velvet was a moving, tearjerker of a film about an enthusiastic, young girl's love for her horse, The Pie, and her firm belief that the auction-won troublemaker could win big in England's famed horserace, the Grand National. In the movie, Elizabeth Taylor was beautiful, earnest, winsome and infectious. She was an intuitive actress, able to summon tears as needed by inhabiting a character's situation. She didn't have any formal acting training (and she would reportedly never get one in her entire life), but she had charisma, and a technique all on her own that managed to get the job done. They were on full display here, and the movie made her a star.

The success of *National Velvet* ushered in yet another larger-than-life Elizabeth Taylor story. She was a teenage sensation, and had asked MGM studio head honcho, Louis B.

Mayer, for drama classes. The known terror allegedly called her stupid, and barked at her about not meddling in how he made movies. She supposedly shot back, telling him he and his studio could "*go to hell.*" Her fire could be attributed to a child's innocence on the kind of power Mayer could wield, but then again, the bursts of brash courage would be apparent even as she got older.

Drama classes or no, like a good working actress and contract player, she went along with typical teenaged fare for a few years afterwards, with great success. She churned out hits including *Courage of Lassie* (1946), *Life with Father* (1947) and *Little Women* (1949), but none of them were particularly challenging for the young actress. She had to rely on her own intuition, her mother's occasionally overbearing coaching, or on tips and practices she gleaned from the people she worked with.

In the meantime, the stunning, violet-eyed beauty with no bad angles was growing up before audiences right on the screens. In no time at all, she was a pocket rocket at 5 feet, 2 inches, with an enviable 19-inch waistline. Changes were soon afoot as to what kinds of parts she could take on as a young actress moving from being a girl to being a woman. It was only a question of when, and what role would be ideal for her. Among the many things that are remarkable about Elizabeth Taylor's career though, is that at a time when most girls of her age in her profession would have been in the awkward stage, she did not encounter that same difficulty with transitioning to adult fare.

In *Little Women* (1949), she was still the youngest of the March girls, Amy. But in *Conspirator* (also 1949), she was (though still young) the wife of a conflicted Communist spy. The leap from child star to emerging leading lady was pretty much seamless. She endeared as a fresh-faced, beautiful, vulnerable child one moment and in the next, she enticed as a voluptuous, sensual young woman.

Behind the scenes, she straddled the line too; she was only 17 years old when filming *The Conspirator*, doing schoolwork but also fielding rather serious advances from older men. Here's another stranger-than-fiction Elizabeth Taylor story – eccentric RKO top dog, Howard Hughes (a Hollywood legend on his own and the subject of no less than Martin Scorsese's *The Aviator*) allegedly offered her parents $1 million for her hand in marriage. She reportedly found it so funny she had to laugh.

Elizabeth Taylor, at any rate, had other millionaire fish to fry. She and 23-year-old Nicky Hilton of *the* Hilton family, were in love. Nicky was the playboy son of hotel tycoon Conrad Hilton, and a marriage between him and the actress meant theirs could very well be the wedding of the year. They were, after all, two of America's hottest, wealthiest and most famous youngsters.

The ever-savvy MGM took the press attention as an opportunity to foist a fitting new movie on the public. Around the same time, they released Vincente Minelli's family comedy, *Father of the Bride* (1950). Elizabeth

Taylor was resplendent in bridal wear as the precious daughter that Spencer Tracy's endearing turn as Stanley Banks has to learn to let go, on top of having to deal with wedding preparation chaos. In a sense, we as the audience were also being conditioned to launch the beloved child actress to another phase in her life, both professionally and personally. She had become a woman of marriageable age, and ready for more mature roles.

The marriage with Nicky Hilton did not quite work out (more on this and Elizabeth Taylor's other romantic misadventures, later), but professionally, Elizabeth Taylor would thereafter be seen in more adult parts. *A Place in the Sun* (1951) was almost a prophetic title for the actress, who made the most notable leap from child star to grown-up roles here. It's as if she skipped the awkward stages and became a stunning woman with depth and gravitas on top of sensuality. In this George Stevens project, she was dreamy debutante Angela Vickers, *almost* as irresistible to the camera as she was to screen partner Montgomery Clift's character, George Eastman. Eastman, after all, had pretty much been ready to commit murder for her love, while the camera only captured her tantalizing beauty.

Her role as Angela Vickers is on par with her star making turn as Velvet Brown in *National Velvet*, as it also marked an important time in her career. With *National Velvet*, she made her name as a child star. In *A Place in the Sun*, she broke through her old image and came into her own as Elizabeth Taylor, a legitimate screen siren. Angela and Velvet are among her best and most memorable performances, which would eventually include:

- Leslie Benedict in *Giant* (1956) – The George Stevens film could have sailed on star wattage alone – Elizabeth Taylor, Rock Hudson and James Dean shared the screen! – but the director would also get an Oscar nod for this sprawling Texas epic about the trials of a wealthy ranching family.

- Maggie the Cat in *Cat on a Hot Tin Roof* (1958) – Elizabeth Taylor wowed as the seductive but loving Maggie Pollitt, in a wonderful adaptation of a Tennessee Williams play. It is a performance loved by her fans, and frequently cited as a case for her acting talents. She would be nominated for an Oscar here.

- Catherine Holly in *Suddenly, Last Summer* (1959), saw Elizabeth Taylor playing a traumatized young woman driven insane by what she had witnessed of her cousin's death during a Spanish holiday. She goes toe to toe against Katherine Hepburn's wealthy and vicious Violet Venable, in this Joseph L. Manckiewicz-helmed film. She would get another Best Actress nomination at the Oscars for this movie.

- As Gloria Wandrous in *Butterfield 8* (1960) – Gloria would bring Taylor her first Oscar, after a succession of nominations. The drama, which also featured her then-husband Eddie Fischer, showed her as a New York call girl on the brink of finding love, except she and her lover are still hounded by her past. Taylor reportedly disliked the film, and not even her Oscar win could redeem it for her. She won the award a few weeks after a severe bout with pneumonia that necessitated an emergency tracheotomy, leading to the belief held by some that her win was partly due to sympathy.

- The title role in *Cleopatra* (1963) – Cleopatra was not her best role or her best movie, but it is almost certainly the most important one in establishing her iconic status. It was the movie that allowed her to command a cool million dollars – the first actress to be paid so much. It was an infamous disaster, with a production diary deserving of its own movie. Just as epic and excessive was the scale of *"Le Scandale"* – for in *Cleopatra*, Elizabeth Taylor fell hard in love for the man she would eventually marry and divorce twice, Richard Burton.

- Martha in *Who's Afraid of Virginia Woolf* (1966) – this was Taylor's second Best Actress Oscar win, with director Mike Nichols at the helm and her beloved Richard Burton again co-starring. Martha was forceful, angry, biting and embittered, a co-perpetrator and co-victim of a dysfunctional marriage laid bare in one alcohol-fueled night.

These roles are commonly regarded as Elizabeth Taylor's most iconic performances, but over the span of almost seven decades in the entertainment industry, with pretty much just as many credits to her filmography as there are years in her career, some projects were more meaningful to her personal life than they were to her professional achievements.

Father of the Bride, for example, had used her real-life wedding to playboy hotelier, Nicky Hilton, as an opportunity to sell more tickets at the box office; the studio even footed the bill. *Love is Better Than Ever* (1952), would put her in the path of her first entanglement with a married man – director and choreographer, Stanley Donen. *Ivanhoe* (1952), the movie she was sent to film in England to get her away from Donen's sphere and a potentially damaging scandal, would lead her to Michael Wilding, who would be her second husband. And of course, in *Cleopatra*, she and Richard Burton created sparks on and off the screen – which they would do repeatedly, sometimes to greatness (as was the case in *Who's Afraid of Virginia Woolf?*) and other times to middling results, over the course of all the work they did together.

Indeed, "Liz and Dick" as the controversial couple would eventually be known, co-starred in 10 feature films, appeared in a hit theater production of the hits-too-close-to-home, *Private Lives*, and of course the most compelling piece of entertainment of them all: the scandal of their love affair.

Liz and Dick were the original tabloid cover couple, setting tongues afire and selling papers aplenty across all corners of the world when they fell in love while both being married to other people. They were a global sensation. But sometimes, lost amid their beauty, shameless glamor and the flouting of convention in the name of passion – we forget how much love they may have had. Tragic, painful, consuming love. Because not only would Richard Burton be husband number five and six, but according to Elizabeth Taylor lore, shortly before his death Burton had written her a last love letter. She would reportedly cherish this letter until her own death; it was kept at her bedside, they say. She never divulged its contents or showed it publicly, and it was supposedly buried with her.

The story made Richard Burton top contender in the public speculation on who could have been Elizabeth Taylor's favorite husband… for she famously had eight marriages to seven men.

Elizabeth Taylor-Hilton-Wilding-Todd-Fisher-Burton-Burton-Warner-Fortensky

Elizabeth Taylor was a romantic.

When she fell in love, she fell hard. She seemed able to win over most any man that spurred her serious interest, but she was a creature seemingly crafted to have a different kind of life from that led by normal people with longstanding relationships and stable families. Reared on the studio, she did not have a normal childhood or much of a chance for a normal relationship with peers. What she may have grown up seeing on set couldn't have been normal either, because cinematic passion and epic drama belonged more to the movies than to the usual life of a husband and wife. But perhaps because she had known no other life, her romantic entanglements would have these in spades.

Her first documented romantic interest was a fellow student, John Derek. It is not known how far that crush progressed. It is also not known how many conquests she ultimately had, for it seemed as if she could have anyone she wanted. What is known, however, is that she had her share of Hollywood hookups and had famously wed eight times – accounting for the train of last names following her maiden "Taylor," a joke that would follow her romantic misadventures.

Her first high profile romance was with blond, blue-eyed, football star, Glenn Davis in 1948. He was a three-time All-American and a 1946 Heisman Trophy winner while playing for the U.S. Military Academy. He had great football skills to match an Olympic sprint, with movie star good looks to boot. For a while he was America's most popular athlete, gracing the cover of *Time* and *Life*. By some accounts, it was Elizabeth Taylor's mother, Sara, who encouraged the couple to date, believing it would have a positive effect on her 16-year-old daughter's image. By some accounts, the relationship was a game, a sham, a put-on show. Other reports say he was truly in love and they were engaged in 1949, but not for long; at any rate, 'the first fiancé of Elizabeth Taylor' is a distinction more closely associated with William Douglas Pawley Jr.

Bill Pawley was the son of wealthy and influential former U.S. Ambassador William Pawley Sr., but he had his own achievements. He was a decorated pilot for the U.S. Army air Corps. He was 28 and she was 17 when they fell in love, when the Taylors vacationed in Florida. The Pawleys had a grand home in Miami Beach. The young couple wrote each other plenty of letters in 1949, which inevitably made their way to the auction houses in the year 2000s–along with a few letters from Elizabeth's mother, who had asked Bill to step back after he and Elizabeth ended their engagement.

Elizabeth's writings to Bill, revealed a young woman very much in love, imagining a marriage of 75 years and having over a dozen great-great-grandchildren. She also expressed her regret and longing when she had to return his ring, at one point reportedly writing, "*… I suppose this will be the last time I have it on…*" and telling Pawley to care for it, because it still held her heart at its center.

According to friends, the engaged couple may have called it quits due to her pursuit of a thriving career, while he may have been angling for someone who was more of a homemaker. Either way, the romance was short-lived and the young heartbreaker was really just beginning her collection of conquests.

Early in her foray into a movie career, Elizabeth caught the eye of eccentric billionaire Howard Hughes, who was much older (he was in his 40s when she was in her late teens). He had already been linked to screen greats, Joan Crawford, Bette Davis, Ava Gardner, Katherine Hepburn and Lana Turner – but was at one point or another, allegedly willing to either foot the bill for a movie studio or hand her parents a million bucks, if they could only arrange a marriage between him and Liz.

It was no temptation for the fiery actress. She was not interested.

Mrs. Hilton (1950)

Barely an adult, she instead married 23-year-old playboy, Nicky Hilton, son of hotelier Conrad Hilton, on the 6th of May, 1950. It was a grand ceremony at the Church of the Good Shepherd in Beverly Hills attended by

600 people, with thousands of fans gathered outside. The $3,500 gown that clung to the young star's enviable curves, was by MGM costume designer Helen Rose – who would later achieve fashion immortality for the dress worn by Grace Kelly when she married the Prince of Monaco in 1956.

Elizabeth Taylor had reportedly entered into the union with an eye toward forever (and some say, an eye toward escaping her restrictive home life), but instead found gambling, heavy drinking, abusive behavior, indifference and mental cruelty. Hilton may have even harmed her enough to cause a miscarriage. He, on the other hand, reportedly felt as if he had "*married an institution*," rather than a girl. It probably didn't help that he was sometimes called "Mr. Taylor."

Their marriage began to crumble quickly, and Elizabeth suffered true heartache from it. She hurt not just mentally but also physically from the setback. She lost a staggering amount of weight, and suffered high blood pressure, colitis and ulcer. She fell into a sorry state, and some have even described her as being on the brink of a breakdown. It wasn't just the broken illusions about the perfect marriage or the forever love; all her life she had been protected from harsh realities and difficulties by her parents and the people who surrounded her and pandered to her as a successful child star. She was not properly equipped with such a stunning disappointment.

She tried to return to how she was before being Mrs. Nicky Hilton. She couldn't return home to her family, for she had been changed by her experiences. She may have also wanted to avoid the pressures Mrs. Taylor allegedly exerted for the marriage to improve, in fear of what a divorce might do to Elizabeth's career. She was reportedly taken in by kind friends during this difficult period. Though haggard and aching she also continued to work, finishing up *Father's Little Dividend* (1951). The studio kept her busy; work was known to offer her solace and escape. But it was also in doing work that she would often find new romance and fresh drama.

Such was the case when she worked on *Love Is Better Than Ever* (1952), directed by 27-year-old Stanley Donen. He was smart and gentle, and she quickly came to depend upon him. He seemed to know how to manage her; he handled her carefully and has reportedly been willing to shut down a set when her nerves failed her, but he also somehow managed to keep their film work moving forward. It was an impressive feat, and Taylor wasn't the only one who liked Donen; the studio found his handling of the situation to be impressive. Indeed, he was a true talent who would go on to work on many great films, including one of the best ones of all time – *Singin' in the Rain* (1952), and he would work with some of Hollywood's most storied talent, like Fred Astaire, Gene Kelly and Audrey Hepburn. His creative vision would even put an honorary Oscar in his hands for his lifetime of achievements. And so, even when he was in his 20s on the set of a so-so movie like *Love Is Better Than Ever*, the general consensus was that Stanley Donen was a good man – just not the right match for Elizabeth Taylor. He was, after all, unavailable. He was married to dancer Jeanne Coyne from 1947 to 1951, while his romance with Liz was at around 1950.

As they began to fall deeper in love, their romance was trailed by inevitable drama. Mrs. Taylor and Elizabeth reportedly argued about her unacceptable lover publicly and even violently. Mrs. Donen for her part, allegedly threatened to name Elizabeth, just fresh from her own marital scandal, as a co-respondent in their divorce. They could be headed for a crisis, and so at the end of filming, the studio finally came upon a solution to keep their entanglement from escalating further.

Mrs. Wilding (1952)

MGM gave their star a role overseas, to play Rebecca Ivanhoe in *Ivanhoe* (1952). Their tactic removed her from the sphere of Stanley Donen, but they placed her in the path of dashing British actor, Michael Wildling. They supposedly met briefly in Hollywood while she was seeing Donen, and Wilding got in touch with her when she arrived to help her in her new surroundings. They had many meals together, and his presence eventually proved almost curative to her ailments. They fell in love.

Michael, however, had more than a few things against him in the eyes of people who had an interest in the "institution" of Elizabeth Taylor. The snobbish sophisticate was 20 years older than her, on top of being the husband of actress, Kay Young (though they were separated). He was also reportedly having an affair with screen legend Marlene Dietrich, on top of having a reputation as a bisexual who allegedly carried on an affair with another fellow actor.

The studio again tried to interfere, setting Taylor up with teen star Tab Hunter, but her sights remained fixed upon the debonair Wilding. She was even the one who proposed to him. Michael reportedly had concerns about their age difference, and about how their feelings might change in the future. When *Ivanhoe* finished filming on location in England, they were able to put their commitment to the test, and set things into motion if they did still end up wanting to be together. Their divorces each run their respective course, and when they met again months later, they were eager for the next step.

They married in London on the 21st of February, 1952. For the short ceremony, she wore another beautiful piece by Helen Rose. The reception was held at Claridge's and like her previous marriage, Liz and her husband were cheered by thousands of fans. Her parents, however, were not in attendance and neither was her brother, Howard, who was in Korea for military service.

Wilding was not as financially secure as Elizabeth, and his quick divorce reportedly had him pinching pennies. But being married to Elizabeth had a wealth of perks, including her footing the bill for their honeymoon, and in Hollywood, helping him secure a sweet salary from MGM that he otherwise would not have been able to command. Their respective film outputs during their marriage was mostly artistically unremarkable, though they did encounter and/or create the occasional Hollywood controversy by rejecting and/or condemning roles and movies they felt inferior or inappropriate to them, and by the airs they put up and lavish spending they made as a couple.

Her star continued to shine though. She was 24, a Hollywood actress still in high demand, and sharing the screen with the likes of young, virile men like Rock Hudson and James Dean in the luscious epic, *Giant* (1956). But around the time of the filming, her romantic life started to decline. It might have been the disparity in the state of their careers. It may also have been their age difference, which, while not a discouraging factor when they first fell in love, the succeeding years may have made their differences more glaring. There were also accusations of extramarital entanglements and inappropriate behavior on both sides.

Some biographers, however, note that as Michael and Elizabeth's marriage struggled, they've increasingly found themselves relying on the company of good friends to help them along. Specifically, Elizabeth's confidant and soul mate, her frequent co-star, Montgomery Clift. The two were filming the multi-million-dollar epic, *Raintree County* (1957) when Clift figured in a horrific car crash near the Wildings' home. The brutal result was mostly to his legendarily beautiful face – severe cuts, fractured jaws, shattered nose. Film production screeched to a halt for weeks, and with Clift incapacitated, the couple had no intermediary, and no good common friend to the couple who could advise Elizabeth Taylor against beginning another affair.

Mrs. Todd (1957)

The marriage scruples of the Wildlings were becoming common knowledge, which allowed bold men to come forward and take their chances with the breathtaking Elizabeth Taylor. But few men were quite as bold and daring as businessman, Mike Todd. He invited them to gatherings and made his move.

Todd was much older than Elizabeth, and older even than her husband, Michael. But he had an energy about him. He was a headstrong, flamboyant, wealthy power player. He knew what he wanted, and he was not afraid to pursue it and pay for it. In this case, he wanted Elizabeth Taylor for himself. A lot of men did, but Mike Todd was lucky enough that Liz liked his style, too – and he had the financial means to constantly amaze her with jewels, flowers, lavish gifts, private plane rides and luxe holidays.

Eventually, Michael Wilding and Elizabeth Taylor divorced amicably. Their union had yielded two sons, both born by C-section, Michael and Christopher (born 1953 and 1955). Part of the agreement Mike Todd had reportedly helped secure, was that the two boys would spend most of the year with their mother.

By the 2nd of February, 1957, Elizabeth Taylor would be standing in another Helen Rose dress, getting married to Mike Todd in Acapulco. Standing by their side at the ceremony were Todd's good friend, the singer and actor, Eddie Fisher as best man. His wife, singer and actress Debbie Reynolds, was the matron of honor. Among the guests this time, were Elizabeth Taylor's parents and her brother.

When he died, it would be revealed that Mike Todd wasn't as scandalously wealthy as he projected. But for a while after their marriage, Elizabeth would have multiple luxe properties in locations such as New York, Connecticut and Palm Springs. He showered her with lavish gifts and was open to the press about proving his love with expensive presents and grand gestures. They were also open about having the occasional loud row, considering it a key and attractive part of their marriage. The couple promoted themselves and Todd's film, *Around the World in Eighty Days* (1956) tirelessly and with much aplomb. Shortly after the marriage, Liz would give birth to a daughter, Liza. The pregnancy was not without risks, and both Elizabeth and the baby almost died. Doctors thereafter advised her against having another child.

Their marriage would end in tragedy. Just a few months after the birth of their daughter, Mike Todd's private plane, the *Lucky Liz*, was caught in a storm and crashed en route to New York. There were no survivors. Elizabeth, who was supposed to have been on the flight except she had to stay home while ill, was so inconsolable and hysterical at the news that she had to be drugged. Amongst the first of the couple's friends to show support was Debbie Reynolds, who stepped in to help with Elizabeth Taylor's children.

Mrs. Fisher (1959)

It hurt very much to be twice-divorced and a widow at the age of 26. In some ways, Elizabeth's marriage to Mike Todd, who had been very controlling and possessive of her, infantilized her. She depended on him heavily in spite of their arguments and fights. It was difficult, but for a survivor like Elizabeth Taylor, life somehow just went on and love, love as always would come again for the irresistible siren.

The only part that was shocking about it, was from whom that love would next come.

The grieving widow, who at the time of her husband's death was at work on *Cat on a Hot Tin Roof*, managed to return to filming after a short break, and gave one of the finest performances of her career. She would be nominated for an Academy Award for her role as Maggie the Cat. While her acting was receiving accolades though, her public image was taking a blow. The marriage between Mike Todd's dear friend, Eddie Fisher, and Fisher's wife, Debbie Reynolds, was on the rocks. And with Fisher and Taylor both hit hard by Mike Todd's death, they both found love in each other.

Elizabeth Taylor was quickly branded a homewrecker for coming in between America's Sweethearts – never mind that the marriage may or may not have been a sham for the press, as would later be alleged, or if it was genuine, that it had already soured. The optics were simply bad; Debbie Reynolds was loved for being the girl next door, and a diamond-draped scarlet woman had stolen her father's children from her.

Not that Eddie and Elizabeth were too discouraged. America's Sweethearts divorced, and Fisher and Taylor married on the 12th of May, 1959 in Nevada. She had converted to the Jewish faith, too. There were real financial consequences to their union, including thousands of complaint letters, bodily threats, bans of Fisher records on stores and eventually, the cancellation of Fisher's TV show. Still, he had a regular gig in Las Vegas, and her career didn't really take a hit either. She not only continued to work, she also received recognition for her acting. She was nominated at the Oscars for her work on *Suddenly, Last Summer* as well as *Butterfield 8*; she would win the latter. As a matter of fact, she had enough cachet to eventually demand $1 million for her next movie, *Cleopatra*.

Eddie Fisher found out the hard way how seemingly unavoidable and difficult it was to become "Mr. Taylor." He was with her for the filming of *Suddenly, Last Summer* – it was part-honeymoon, and he was allegedly distrustful of Mankiewicz. Taylor campaigned for him to have a role in *BUtterfield 8*, and by the time they started filming for *Cleopatra*, he was reportedly on the studio (Fox, now) payroll as a kind of secretary, with tasks including keeping his unpredictable and feisty wife sober and ready for work. Her multiple health issues were also consuming him. The overwhelming, immersive experience of being Elizabeth Taylor's husband, coupled with his own career becoming de-prioritized, as well as each of their own temperaments and personalities, slowly brought their marriage to its death throes.

The scene was set for a new player to enter the scene: Richard Burton.

Mrs. Burton (1964-1974); (1975 - 1976)

To say that *Cleopatra* was a troubled production is a deep and profound understatement. In many ways, it became a turning point for both Hollywood and for its leading lady, the million-dollar actress, Elizabeth Taylor.

The original goals 20th Century Fox had set for *Cleopatra* was a compact $2 million film slated for release in March, 1960. Producer Walter Wanger eventually imagined a larger movie - an epic. He pitched his idea to studio heads, Buddy Adler and Spyros P. Skouras. The actress he tapped to play the lead was larger-than-life too, and she commanded a salary to match – a $1 million guarantee. Little did they know that the scale of the movie's vision and the demands of its lead actress would be matched by proportionate production drama and critical and commercial disappointment.

Eventually, the studio came to an agreement with their Cleopatra, Elizabeth Taylor. She reportedly had $125,000 weekly for 16 weeks, plus $50,000 afterwards, plus 10% of the movie's gross, along with $3,000 weekly in living expenses along with an allowance for first class plane tickets and food and lodging. It was an unprecedented deal, but she was just one of many trials in a troubled production.

The script was not finalized. Filming in England proved disastrous, with restrictive unions and Pinewood Studios having structural and technological limitations that were ill-fitting to the project. Costumes and sets were not ready. The English weather made the lead actress ill, and the steam from the cold climate was distinctly *not* Egyptian. Elizabeth Taylor's illness grew worse, commanding the attention of the Queen's personal physician. In the meantime, these and other delays were costing the studios millions over millions of dollars – which would balloon with a change of directors.

Rouben Mamoulian stepped down, and Joseph Mankiewicz stepped in. Securing his commitment and buying him out of other obligations had piled on to the additional, unexpected costs.

Bringing Mankiewicz to the project set stage for even more costly changes, including a new script. A more serious illness befell Elizabeth Taylor too – acute staphylococcus pneumonia – that brought her to death's door. She rallied with the help of a tracheotomy, but the incident cost the troubled production another six months. Not that she was the only problem; when they finally started filming again, the circus had relocated to Italy and some of the main players had changed – Caesar was now Rex Harrison and Anthony was to be played by Tony Award-winning Welsh talent, Richard

Burton. But the script was still troublesome and unfinished, which did not allow for comprehensive production planning. Sets and costumes were either incomplete or just ready and idly waiting; with no master plan the director shot whatever was on the page costing time and film; extras waited around without doing anything, getting paid for their time; and Mankiewicz was working himself to the ground, directing by day and writing by night. Richard Burton and Elizabeth Taylor's romance would only add to the production's headaches.

Burton, like Taylor, was married during filming. He had 12 years of marriage with his first wife, Sybil, and they had two children, but he was no saint; he had acquired a reputation for entanglements with his leading ladies. He wasn't a fan of Taylor at the onset and was skeptical of her acting prowess. She, on the other hand, knew he had talent but did not like his personality. Over the course of working together though, there was an electricity between the two actors that powered their scenes. "*Le Scandale*" would soon be recognized on set, known the world over, and merit the denouncement of Congress and the Vatican.

Cleopatra wasn't just a cornerstone for filmmaking, it was also a cornerstone for the public conception of celebrity and sexuality. Paparazzi culture was in its infancy, and Liz & Dick were the ideal subjects to help it thrive. It was also the 1960s; the sexual revolution. Things that would have been once swept beneath the rug in a more restrictive time were coming out into the open – including passionate sex and lavish love affairs – and clashing with more established mores. And while the couple received condemnation, they kicked and bucked and stayed together. Later, they would actually be sued by the producers of *Cleopatra* for millions in damages, and included the claim that the couple's irresponsible conduct off-screen had been damaging to the film and was a breach of their contract.

At least the publicity of the affair managed to draw in curious crowds at the box office. When the mammoth, 220+-minute *Cleopatra* was released in 1963, it was one of the highest grossing films of the year. The critics at the time were generally unhappy with it, but the movie would still get the Oscar nod on multiple categories, including wins for Art Direction, Cinematography, Costume

Design, and Visual Effects. The price tag was still high, though – from a dreamy budget of $2 million they reportedly went up to $30 on production and $15 in promotions (or about $320 million total if adjusted for current value of money). The film would recoup losses only years later when millions were paid for it to be shown on television in 1966. The project nearly brought the studio to ruin, and pretty much killed off others' incentive to gamble with the genre of big budget epics in the future.

On a lighter note – at least it gave us one of the greatest love stories of all time (or so it seemed). Burton and Taylor divorced their spouses and were married in Canada on March, 1964. They commanded top dollar together, and from 1964 to 1972, reportedly managed to earn $50 million together (even if the quality of their filmography at this time was questionable). They were a beautiful, successful and shamelessly lavish couple. Among Burton's most memorable presents? The 33.19-carat Krupp diamond, which would eventually be attached to Elizabeth Taylor's name.

Theirs was a passionate union, but not at all an easy one. They had to contend with constant, frenzied public attention, yes – in Boston for example, Elizabeth suffered her chunks of her hair pulled off, as well as a bloodied ear missing an earring, while Richard's sleeve was lost in the melee. But mostly, they had to contend with each other.

He reportedly continued to feel guilt over how his first marriage ended. She, on the other hand, was paranoid of his female co-stars. Their fights became more frequent and escalated. It was said that when they took hotel rooms, they would get two so as not to disturb other guests with their loud arguments. It was also reported that Richard Burton's impressive intellect and command of language became even more pronounced when he gave her brutal, verbal lashings with his sharp tongue. Things were not helped at all by heavy drinking. Over the years they both descended into alcohol abuse. Finally, towards the end of their decade together, Burton's long-dormant roving eye started acting up again. They announced a split on Independence Day, 1974.

They would be drawn together again and again though, and she in particular had aggressively courted him back. They remarried, but divorced again after just a few months. The marriage still didn't work out, but they remained more or less in each other's lives afterward. They married other people; Senator John Warner of Virginia for Liz, and model Susan Hunt for Burton. But had kept in some contact and retained some affection for each other.

In 1983, their interactions still contained that magical spark, and when Elizabeth Taylor's theater company planned a stage revival of the play, *Private Lives*, they looked to project that spark before theater audiences. The play was about ex-couple, Elyot and Amanda, who had just left their new spouses to give each other another try. Reviews were so-so, but the show got them $70,000 weekly, and it was a hit, drawing in the crowds as Taylor and Burton unsurprisingly still could. There were even rumors of another re-marriage (Elizabeth Taylor and John Warner were already divorced at this time), quickly foiled when Burton married his girlfriend, Sally Hay.

He died the following year in August, 1984, of a cerebral hemorrhage in his sleep. Elizabeth Taylor was hysterical at news of his loss, and the magnitude of her hurts reportedly cost her her engagement to Victor Luna, a Mexican lawyer who could have been husband number eight.

Shortly before he died, Richard Burton supposedly wrote Liz a 'last love letter.' This infamous piece of paper with its secret contents basically was supposed to say that Elizabeth Taylor was his home, and that he wanted to return home.

This is unverified, and for now, unverifiable. Richard Burton's widow, Sally Burton, denied the existence of such a letter. It may have even been an invention of Elizabeth Taylor's, or her or Burton's biographers, or any of the starry-eyed fans and romantics who wanted a bit of lingering hope to end one of the greatest love affairs of all time.

It is one more story in the larger than life legend of Elizabeth Taylor.

Mrs. Warner (1976)

Liz's career peaked in the 1960s and quieted by the 1970s and 1980s. It was at this time that she fell in love and married Virginia Senator and former Navy secretary, John Warner. They wed at his Virginia farm on the 4th of December, 1976. She was 44 years old, but still dazzling people everywhere she went – including the jaded folks of the political power set in Washington. But home was their farm in Virginia, where she played the devoted wife, championing him in the press, cooking for him and being an ideal hostess. She enjoyed the country life, and would even be spotted shopping in the community. Her husband, however, was a very busy man – she got lonely and bored by some accounts. According to other reports, she couldn't handle the pressure of life as a political wife. Either way, they divorced in 1982, but remained friends afterwards.

Mrs. Fortensky (1991)

In the 1980s, her notoriously tenuous health was also impaired by a dependence on alcohol and drugs. She was heavily into painkillers to control the anguish from a multitude of collected illnesses and injuries, especially on her back. She checked into rehab, where she met husband number eight in 1988.

Larry Fortensky, he of the unforgettable last name, was a construction worker 20 years younger than the iconic star. He was in rehab for alcohol, and had the most unbelievable background for a spouse of the Queen of Hollywood. The difference between her lifestyle and his working class background seemed to have been breached by her sweetness and good humor. She called him "Larry the lion" and liked that he had no airs or pretenses about him. Like most people who were not living under a rock, he knew perfectly well who she was, even if he did not watch her films. But what he found attractive was that she was warm and engaging. He loved her childlike enthusiasm, while for her, he was different from other men that she had known and it was refreshing. They had an immediate attraction.

Just as strange as the circumstances that drew them together, they wed in Michael Jackson's Neverland Ranch in 1991. They were together for five years and were generally happy. He never bothered to compete with her, and she indulged him with grand presents that he claimed never to have asked for or encouraged – among the many presents were a Harley, a BMW and jewelry. For his part, he gave her chocolate covered roses and pets. They enjoyed long motorcycle rides, where she could wear a helmet and be anonymous as they headed to distant, quiet beer and burger stops.

He never quite adjusted to the spotlight that trailed her though, and he actually tried to continue to working on a construction site, where she would send meals prepared by a chef via a limo. Eventually, he had to take on the role of "Mr. Taylor" too, trailing her around the world. They were both increasingly unhappy, and they divorced amicably in 1996.

'The Lion' reportedly took home 1 million pounds from her considerable, 200 million-pound fortune, and slinked back into his quiet, somewhat reclusive life. He never succumbed to offers for a kiss-and-tell, even when he suffered medical crises and ran low on funds. She would send him money unbidden though, and they kept in such contact that he would even have a phone call with her the day before she checked into the hospital for the last time. When she died, she is said to have left him 500,000 pounds in her will. He broke his silence only after lies came up about their relationship following her death in 2011. She never married after him, and so after all the glamorous men that made up Elizabeth Taylor's marital history, it was ultimately the somewhat obscure, mysterious and publicity-shy Mr. Fortensky who would forever carry the distinction of being Elizabeth Taylor's last husband.

Legacy of a Survivor

Elizabeth Taylor's friendships were firmer than most of her love affairs. As a friend, she wasn't just loyal and devoted, she was courageous.

Rock Hudson became a lifelong friend from the time they stared together in *Giant*. They were drinking buddies, and not at all unlike a marriage vow, they were bound together 'in sickness and in health.' She visited him in the hospital in the 1980s when he was diagnosed with AIDS, at a time when such a diagnosis inspired fear in so many people. She reportedly snuck in with famed immunologist Dr. Michael Gottlieb, to see him. She worried that hugging and kissing him would harm his health given his compromised immune system; she was not worried for herself. When he died in 1985, she arranged a memorial celebrating his life, featuring mariachis and serving margaritas. His loss inspired her to organize AIDS fundraisers, and eventually she co-founded amfAR for AIDS research. Her Elizabeth Taylor AIDS Foundation, which provides care for people with HIV, funnels millions to hundreds of organizations all over the world.

Her other great friendship was with Montgomery Clift, with whom she became close while filming *A Place in the Sun*. He would have her bravely by his side in at least two very important moments of his life. Around the time they were filming *Raintree County* (1957), he got into a terrible car crash that damaged his face. She reportedly ran to the site of the accident and removed dislodged teeth from inside his throat to keep him from choking. He became scarred and troubled afterwards, but she would champion his casting alongside her for a film two years later, an adaptation of Tennessee Williams' *Suddenly, Last Summer* (1959). They were thick as thieves, and she inspired the same level of devotion from "Monty." He was her sounding board, a consultant in her marriage prospects. He doted on her children, and was reportedly very protective of them. He kept a mini nursery in his New York home, and was said to be disapproving of Elizabeth's affairs if they adversely affected her children.

Speaking of her children – Elizabeth Taylor had a total of four of them. Two sons with second husband, Michael Wildling; her daughter Liza by tragic husband number three, Mike Todd; and adopted daughter, Maria, with Richard Burton. Of the supporting figures within Elizabeth Taylor's legend, they seem to exist quietly in the background. Part of it could have been because her siren image did not quite jive with being a mother so we as a public never quite got used to attaching them to visions of her. Part of it could have been that her love affairs overshadowed them, or that the demands of her career prevented her from being hands-on. She may have also tried to keep them away from the limelight, and let them determine their own course in life as she was not free to do when she was younger.

Either way, she became more like a friend than a disciplinarian parent; she was, after all, barely more than a child herself when she had her first son. She was protective of them though, and because she couldn't be with them all the time, they grew up around assistants, nannies and security. She managed to make time to give them great holiday celebrations and happy memories, though. Her four children were there when she was deemed a Dame of the British Empire in 2000... they were also together for her funeral in 2011. She had passed away at age 79, from congestive heart failure.

Elizabeth Taylor's Goodbye

In the later years of her life, the ever-savvy Elizabeth Taylor wasn't a bankable film star anymore, but she continued to be visible in television, her charity work and through her bestselling perfume and jewelry business.

She also managed to stay in the headlines due to her frail health.

Acting. Marriages. Diamonds… if there is one other thing Elizabeth Taylor was well known for, it was her litany of medical issues and health crises. She didn't just survive the ravages of Hollywood and remained working right up to her 70s – she was a literal survivor, who had weathered a number of near-death experiences that could have sent many people to their knees. They were so plentiful that they could sometimes be baffling, and when one thinks of Elizabeth Taylor simply winning the life lottery on looks, wealth and fame – it is the state of her health that was a constant reminder that this was still a woman who had to fight to keep her place in the world.

This may have started as early as her birth. The double lashes that have framed her famous violet peepers? They were caused by a genetic mutation that had links to heart problems. She was also said to have been born with scoliosis, and would suffer from back problems throughout her life. She wasn't spared from work-related injury either, including a broken foot during *Lassie Come Home*, a horsing accident during *National Velvet* and an eye injury that required surgery during *Elephant Walk* (1954). An injury on vacation with her husband Mike Todd would also necessitate serious surgery to repair her back.

She had a history of nervous breakdowns or near breakdowns too, accompanied by illnesses like colitis and ulcer that trailed the unhappy or traumatic experiences of her life.

Complications from otherwise normal illnesses often found her as well, and over the course of her life, she would be in and out of hospitals for appendicitis, tonsillitis, kidney and bronchial problems, amoebic dysentery, an ovarian cyst and meningism partially caused by an abessed tooth. Severe bouts with pneumonia threatened her life, and serious other issues included a benign brain tumor and skim cancer. She had to go into rehab for a drug dependency that was likely cultivated from her medical history of constant pain from illness and injury. She had hip replacement surgery and was wheelchair-bound toward the final years.

She was a survivor through and through, though. She remained focused and feisty. She had a tendency to beat the odds, outliving even some of those who had once needed to take care of her. Aside from her volatile health, she lived through the ebbs and flows of Hollywood. She survived movies, television and theater, tabloid scandal, an epic flop, and the highs and lows of romance and heartbreak. She survived stardom, and survived aging. When she died she left behind an impressive estate, so that even her finances survived her own vices and her luxurious lifestyle. Elizabeth Taylor knew how to land on her feet. Before she died, she'd even adapted to social media and was an avid user of Twitter!

Her legacy also seems to be surviving her death and all the decades that have come after it. She remains a well-loved figure for her beauty, her talent, her fire, her eccentricity, her electricity, her sheer originality.

An Ever Shining Star

One of the most important contributions Elizabeth Taylor made to the world, was the productive and meaningful use of her beauty, fame and talents for charitable causes. She was, as was earlier mentioned, a loyal friend and a woman who was generous with love. It was her friendships that inspired her activism, which in turn would yield millions in research and relief for HIV and AIDS sufferers all over the world. She was a good mother and a good grandmother too, and had an infectious passion for doing charity. She became a lightning rod of inspiration particularly for her grandchildren and great-grandchildren – and a number of them continue her work through the Elizabeth Taylor Trust, and find its purpose, as well as that of her other charities, as a unifying force for their extraordinary family. In this way, even in death, she continues to share her light.

Scientifically speaking, some stars are so distant from the Earth that by the time their light reaches us, many have long since come and gone. This lends a more contemplative angle to the title, "Movie Star-" a person we see only from afar, so distant from us that we do not even know if what we see is true or even still there. Few can fit this pensive description more than Elizabeth Taylor, the penultimate Movie Star. She was so outsize in life, that her presence lingers on and looks able to continue to do so, long after her death. We don't even know what is true and what is legend, but her star continues to shine, powered by what she had allowed us to see when she was alive.

And what a beautiful sight this bright star is in the night.

Printed in Great Britain
by Amazon